THE COMMUNITY RECONSTRUCTS

THE COMMUNITY RECONSTRUCTS

The Meaning of Pragmatic
Social Thought

JAMES CAMPBELL

UNIVERSITY OF ILLINOIS PRESS
Urbana and Chicago

This book is printed on acid-free paper.

Library of Congress Cataloging-in-Publication Data

Campbell, James, 1948-
    The community reconstructs : the meaning of pragmatic social
thought / James Campbell.
        p.   cm.
    Includes bibliographical references and index.
    ISBN 0-252-01842-7 (alk. paper).—ISBN 0-252-06207-8 (alk. paper
: pbk.)
    1. Pragmatism. 2. Social sciences—Philosophy. I. Title.
B944.P72C36   1992
300'.1—dc20   91-3020
                                                                  CIP

For Annamarie—
at the beginning of adulthood.

CONTENTS

PREFACE

This study of the social aspects of American Pragmatism has both historical and social goals. The former center around the complexities of recovering a fuller understanding of our intellectual past; the latter, around the complexities of building a better future. That these two sets of goals should be connected is the thesis of this volume.

I have been working on themes in Pragmatic social thought for some time, and earlier versions of several of the following chapters have appeared elsewhere: chapter 2, "William James and the Ethics of Fulfillment," *Transactions of the C. S. Peirce Society* 17, no. 3 (Summer 1981): 224–40; chapter 3, "George Herbert Mead on Intelligent Social Reconstruction," *Symbolic Interaction* 4, no. 2 (Fall 1981): 191–205; chapter 4, "Dewey's Method of Social Reconstruction," *Transactions of the C. S. Peirce Society* 20, no. 4 (Fall 1984): 363–93; chapter 5, "Politics and Conceptual Reconstruction," *Philosophy and Rhetoric* 17, no. 3 (Summer 1984): 156–70, copyright 1984 by the Pennsylvania State University, reproduced by permission of the Pennsylvania State University Press; chapter 7, "Optimism, Meliorism, Faith," *History of Philosophy Quarterly* 4, no. 1 (January 1987): 93–113; and chapter 8, "Philosophers and the Nature of Wisdom," *Metaphilosophy* 22, nos. 1–2 (January–April 1991): 41–49. I am grateful for permission to reprint them here.

I am grateful as well for the assistance that I have received over the years, from teachers and friends too numerous to mention, understanding the social themes of American Pragmatism. Preeminent among these is John J. McDermott, whose editorial endeavors have simplified the task of all who would understand Pragmatism, and whose lectures and essays have increased the numbers of such individuals tremendously.

1

Introduction:
Pragmatic Social Thought

There has been a great deal of interest lately in the meaning of American Pragmatism. Ironically, however, up to now this interest has generally confined itself to intellectualistic topics—important, but not transcendently important, topics like Pragmatism's understanding of meaning and truth, its relationship to semiotics and foundationalism, its commitments to naturalism and realism—to the exclusion of Pragmatic social thought.[1] I do not mean to suggest that the social thought of the two key figures in this movement, John Dewey and George Herbert Mead, has been completely neglected. On the contrary, each figure has been a source of ideas and challenges, and the object of repudiation and revision as well. What has been sadly neglected in the discussions of Dewey and Mead, however, is their connection with each other and with other Pragmatic social thinkers and how this movement is situated within the larger context of American social life. It is these gaps that I attempt to bridge in this volume.

Dewey and Mead and others, like their colleague James Hayden Tufts, grew to consciousness in the ferment of Progressive America and attempted to use the burgeoning university as a means to the amelioration of social ills. By employing the power of the new sciences of society—anthropology and sociology, psychology and education—they hoped to overcome society's deadness of habit and tradition so that it could begin to face its problems "intelligently." We are now, of course, more skeptical about the power and the objectivity of the tools they had at their disposal. This skepticism, however, need not cause us to automatically repudiate their goal. I suggest this because, even more than its emphasis upon science, what gave Pragmatic social thought its power was its focus upon the nature and role of institutions in our collective life. Unless we are prepared to deny the possibility of significant change through the cooperative reconstruction of our social institutions, we must grant that the goal of Pragmatic social thought to help society face its problems more intelligently remains at least a possible one; and, if we accept their claim that these problems should be addressed, we are obligated to try. While the topic of Pragmatic social thought requires much more future exploration, this volume provides an introductory sketch of the larger picture.

II

Pragmatism, as a philosophical movement, was continuous with the rest of developing American society, and it needs to be distinguished from at least two other pragmatic strains. One of these is rooted in the practicality and simplicity of the notoriously pragmatic American people. In part, this pragmatism reflects a suspicion of matters intellectual as being generally useless; in part, it reflects the ever-present task of building a new country. The second strain of pragmatic thought in American society, one that is more or less strong in all societies, is the shallow opportunism of the self-styled pragmatists who are concerned only with personal victory regardless of the field of endeavor. Distinct from these two strains is philosophical Pragmatism—the work of Peirce, James, Dewey, Mead, and others—a perspective that developed around a theory of meaning and a theory of truth, and one that sought to ground its efforts in a vision of an adequate human existence. As it matured, Pragmatism offered a metaphysics emphasizing process and relations, a naturalistic and evolutionary understanding of human existence, an analysis of intellectual activity as problem-oriented and as benefiting from historically developed methods, and an emphasis upon the democratic reconstruction of society through educational and other institutions. While it is possible to trace the roots of philosophical Pragmatism back into the history of American philosophy and further still into the Western philosophical tradition,[2] and although some valuable earlier flowerings of American Pragmatism can be identified,[3] I will begin my general survey of this movement with a brief look at Peirce and James.

Charles Sanders Peirce (1839–1914) was a mathematical and scientific genius of the first order who, for reasons both personal and social, came late to public recognition from the philosophical and broader intellectual community.[4] Peirce describes his own work at one point as "the attempt of a physicist to make such conjecture as to the constitution of the universe as the methods of science may permit, with the aid of all that has been done by previous philosophers." His hope is not for demonstrable truths but for likely hypotheses that grow out of science's past efforts and that would be "capable of being verified or refuted by future observers."[5] These observers are, of course, us; and, for Peirce, we are at our best when we are engaged in cooperative attempts to overcome intellectual problems. And, in accordance with his belief that "the opinion which is fated to be ultimately agreed to by all who investigate, is what we mean by the truth,"[6] at each particular point in the ongoing process of cooperative inquiry the individual is admonished to maintain an attitude of hesitancy and openness. "Do not block the way of inquiry," he writes.[7] In our lives as inquirers, we are to adopt a cautious attitude that he calls "fallibilism." Among its tenets are the following points: we should never assume that particular questions are unanswerable, nor that proffered answers are absolutely true, nor that some formulations are final, nor that some level of examination is ultimate, and so on. In inquiry, there is always more to be done; even a failed experiment is an advance since all possibilities must be considered at some point. The great human weakness that we need to avoid is our willingness to settle issues too soon by acquiescing to inadequate methods for the fixation of belief.[8]

Another important theme in Peirce's Pragmatism is his belief that we could learn to be more precise in our philosophical formulations if we could develop an adequate theory of meaning. The focus of his efforts was to clarify our use of "intellectual concepts" or "of hard words and of abstract concepts" like 'hard', 'weight', 'force', and 'reality'.[9] He writes, "A *conception,* that is, the rational purport of a word or other expression, lies exclusively in its conceivable bearing upon the conduct of life; so that, since obviously nothing that might not result from experiment can have any direct bearing upon conduct, if one can define accurately all the conceivable experimental phenomena which the affirmation or denial of a concept could imply, one will have therein a complete definition of the concept."[10] The important points of Peirce's theory of meaning encapsulated here, in addition to the connection to long-term, group inquiry, are that he is interested in applying it only to certain words or concepts and that he requires a consideration of all effects. The weaknesses that Peirce's version of Pragmatism displays, from James's point of view, are the same: it focuses too narrowly on the issues of the natural and formal sciences, and it emphasizes too strongly the public forum of verification.

William James (1842–1910) saw himself as carrying forward Peirce's Pragmatism, although he formulated it more broadly to facilitate its application to ending apparently insoluble philosophical controversies.[11] "The pragmatic method," he writes, "is primarily a method of settling metaphysical disputes that otherwise might be interminable." Although the example that he uses is the homey one of the squirrel circling the tree, the issues to which he thinks the method can be applied are matters of larger human concern, like the questions of substance and attributes, materialism versus theism, and freedom versus determinism. "The prag-matic method in such cases is to try to interpret each notion by tracing its respective practical consequences," he continues. "What difference would it practically make to anyone if this notion rather than that notion were true?"[12] Although this concern with results is continuous with Peirce's work, the changes are fundamental and deliberate.[13] James, maintaining that "the principle of pragmatism . . . should be expressed more broadly than Mr. Peirce expresses it," eliminates the concern with long-term effects for the group and with the full spectrum of effects. "The effective meaning of any philosophic proposition can always be brought down to some particular consequence, in our future practical experience."[14]

In addition, James went further and brought into a central position in his Pragmatism the topic of truth. For James, Pragmatism should have something to say about not only the *meaning* but also about the *meaningfulness,* and ultimately about the *truth or falsity,* of philosophic positions. For example, the conflicting answers to the question of ma-terialism versus theism yield what he calls "opposite outlooks of ex-perience." According to James, "Materialism means simply the denial that the moral order is eternal, and the cutting off of ultimate hopes; theism means the affirmation of an eternal moral order and the letting loose of hope."[15] In deciding between these two outlooks, Peirce's em-phasis upon what is fated to be recognized in the long run by the limitless group of belief-suspending inquirers would seem to be of little help. James, as might be surmised from his emphasis on hope, maintains that a position may be considered to be true as the result of a different kind of test: "Any idea upon which we can ride, so to speak; any idea that will carry us prosperously from any one part of our experience to any other part, linking things satisfactorily, working securely, simplifying, saving labor; is true for just so much, true in so far forth, true *instru-mentally.*"[16] For James, an idea or a philosophical position is true if it satisfies this test of workability. To use, as an example, a question close to James's heart, if the theistic viewpoint provides what he calls *"a value for concrete life,"* it will be true, he writes, *"in the sense of being good for so much."*[17]

Because of his enthusiastic championing of this unorthodox position on truth, James became the center of the storm over Pragmatism. Many important issues related to his understanding of the topic of truth must be passed over here, however, because they would only lead us astray.[18] The one significant problem with James's position on truth from the point of view of Pragmatic social thought is that, in Peircean terms, James allows people to "fix belief", too soon, on the basis of limited evidence or only individual confirmation. As an example of this impulsiveness, we can consider the following: "A new opinion counts as 'true' just in proportion as it gratifies the individual's desire to assimilate the novel in his experience to his beliefs in stock."[19] The weakness of James's approach here is that it does not sufficiently refine the felt problem or adequately evaluate the proposed solution. Recognizing the accuracy of the vernacular expression that many views "contain a little truth," we should be more hesitant, more skeptical; we should test our new opinion in other contexts and consult with other inquirers. We need to be more cautious in the face of the recognition that, as Peirce writes, all too often "as soon as a firm belief is reached we are entirely satisfied, whether the belief be true or false."[20] James's weakness here is not, of course, that he would knowingly call the false "true." It is, rather, that he would call the workable "true" without sufficient testing to make sure that it was not false. And here, as Peirce points out, we need a higher standard.

III

We may now turn to the Social Pragmatists who attempted to combine the inquiring and critical spirit of Peirce with a focus on the issues of general and direct human concern that interested James. John Dewey (1859–1952) is historically the most important figure in this movement and the primary figure in this volume.[21] His methods were critical and cooperative, like Peirce's, but his interests were moral and humanistic, like James's. This generally scientific approach to generally moral issues is made possible by what Dewey called his "Instrumentalism," his attempt to apply the gains of Pragmatism to practical judgments. The "fundamental idea" of the various strands of the Pragmatic movement, Dewey writes, is "that action and opportunity justify themselves only to the degree in which they render life more reasonable and increase its value" (LW 2:19). With this Instrumentalism offering, as it does, a kind of logic of practical activity, Dewey hopes to use it to foster social reconstruction. By means of this Instrumentalism he attempts to recast the question of truth that entangled James to emphasize inquiry, focusing on "warranted assertion" rather than belief or knowledge.[22] But, at the same time, Dewey emphasizes the broad application of this Instrumentalism to the reconstruction of social institutions in order to create more reasonable and valuable lives for all. This is the basis of his efforts in areas as diverse as economic policy and legal practice, educational theorizing and political organization.

George Herbert Mead (1863–1931), Dewey's colleague at the Universities of Michigan and Chicago from 1891 to 1904, is most widely known for his discussion of the phases of the self.[23] The "me" is that phase of the self that contains its social roots. "We are individuals born into a certain nationality, located at a certain spot geographically, with such and such family relations, and such and such political relations," Mead tells us. "All of these represent a certain situation which constitutes the 'me'." (MSS 182). It is this aspect of the self that enables us to take the attitudes of others; moreover, when organized as "the generalized other," the "me" accounts for the individual's "unity of self" (MSS 154). The "I" phase of the self is what Mead calls its possibility to transcend this rootedness. "The 'I' is the response of the individual to the attitude of the community as this appears in his own experience" (MSS 196). To be able to function as an individual member of a community at any given time, it is necessary that the person's self contain both aspects existing in a creative balance: the "me" bringing forth the possible ways of the community and the "I" evaluating and choosing among them. And, Mead maintains, for this balance to continue through time, it is necessary to have an adequate system of egalitarian institutions. Building upon these basic insights, Mead and the other Social Pragmatists constructed a valuable communal perspective to undergird social reconstruction.

James Hayden Tufts (1862–1942) is an important figure, although one lesser known than Dewey or Mead.[24] He was a colleague of both, teaching with Dewey at Michigan (1889–91) and Chicago (1894–1904), and with Mead at Chicago (1894–1930). Throughout his extensive writings runs an emphasis upon the fundamental importance of institutions in human life and their three main characteristics. First, Tufts noted, our institutions are human creations, developed out of simpler and less effective ones. Our evolving family structures and health care systems, for example, are modes of cooperative action designed to address recurring difficulties in our shared lives. Second, our institutions are deliberately modifiable over time to deal with change. "A characteristic of an institution," he writes, "is that while conserving a large measure of what experience has taught it also faces new situations and conflicting interests or forces under a necessity of partial readjustment." Third, institutions have an aim: they are means devised to approach more closely our ideal of a good society. Satisfying this aim requires the ongoing reconstruction of these very institutions. Tufts finds a clear example in the case of our legal institutions, which serve not only to "protect stability" but also to "adjust to change."[25] In our deliberations to establish and maintain justice in our changing world, he writes, we need to consider "not merely the principles recognized in the seventeenth and eighteenth centuries, but the emerging principles of the twentieth."[26] In Tufts's rejection of the view that current social justice can be found in conformity to past arrangements, even if these arrangements were at the time just,and elsewhere in his discussions of social reconstruction, we see the application of the evolutionary worldview of Pragmatic social thought to the problems of the contemporary situation.

IV

In the seven chapters that follow I take up the themes of Pragmatic social thought in a manner that is, admittedly, incomplete but still thorough enough to present an adequate picture of the movement. This picture suggests some of the possible values that can be drawn from Pragmatic social thought for our contemporary attempts at social reconstruction, and it hints at the kind of work that still needs to be done. In chapter 2, "William James and the Ethics of Fulfillment," I consider James's moral thought in the context of two conflicting ethical themes. The first of these is the moral importance of personal fulfillment through the choice of options free from external interference, and it is necessarily individualistic; the second is the moral importance of fostering the institutional means necessary to create a good society through cooperative efforts at reform, and it is necessarily social. Not only does the latter theme, which connects ethics and social reform, lie at the core of Pragmatic social thought, it is a necessity for our present situation. Only by turning to the direct examination of questions of social ethics can we hope to foster greater human well-being.

In chapter 3, "George Herbert Mead on Intelligent Social Reconstruction," I consider the position that not only are such reform activities needed, they can be carried on in a fairly intelligent fashion to maximize responsiveness and minimize unexpected consequences. I explore Mead's analysis of the *promise* of a progressive society and also its *basis* in our social existence, our ongoing need for reconstruction, and our possibilities for the communal development of values. In chapter 4, "John Dewey's Method of Social Reconstruction," I consider in fairly close detail Dewey's suggestions about how this social reform might become a reality. Here I maintain that the ongoing importance of Dewey's contribution is to be found not in his specific policy recommendations but rather in his adumbration of a social method for developing, publicizing, and evaluating suggested modes of action. His goal here is the creation of a vibrant democratic society that addresses its ills through cooperative inquiry.

The next three chapters, chapters 5 through 7, are less directly historical. In these chapters I apply aspects of Pragmatic social thought to the context of our day in an attempt to judge the potential value of the Pragmatic analysis. In chapter 5, "Politics and Conceptual Reconstruction," I examine the role of language in the process of social reconstruction. My underlying intention is to develop a response to the current resurgence of reactionary political thinking that travels under the guise of phrases like "original intent." From the point of view of Pragmatic social thought, the practical meaning of terms like *equality* or *democracy* must be understood hypothetically, relative to our current situation; consequently, how we conduct our lives together should be decided by cooperative inquiry, not determined by some process of linguistic archeology. The basis of this Pragmatic response is the recognition of our place in an evolutionary world that requires adjustments in principles as time goes on to maintain and advance the level of human well-being.

In chapter 6, "Freedom and Community," I consider the nature of freedom and its relationship to human fulfillment from the same evolutionary standpoint. In response to our current social situation, where democracy has been virtually equated with freedom, I reject the views that freedom means no more than the elimination of restraints upon individual action and that human fulfillment is to be sought through a single-minded pursuit of this freedom. Instead, I offer a position grounded in Pragmatic social thought that reconnects freedom with equality and presents as the democratic goal the freedom for social individuals to participate equally in the life of the community.

In chapter 7, "Optimism, Meliorism, Faith," I consider the role of the much-brandished notion of realism in social life. My first concern is to distinguish the optimistic belief that all will be well from the melioristic view of Pragmatic social thought that we have in our power the means that may improve our situation. Second, I attempt to elaborate the factors—including our own actions and the level of our faith in our democratic possibilities—that will influence the likelihood of intelligent social reconstruction either way.

Finally, I offer a parting challenge in chapter 8, "Philosophers and the Nature of Wisdom," that arises from this consideration of faith in democracy. It is the position of Pragmatic social thought that the problems of society are both real and amenable to intelligent, cooperative action. Consequently, it is important that intellectuals reconsider the nature of their work on an ongoing basis to determine to what extent their efforts are, or are not, contributing to advancing the social good. This task is especially important for philosophers, who are often drawn by the intoxicating allure of a contemplative sense of wisdom. Pragmatic social thought, with its moral understanding of wisdom and its analysis of the human as rooted in nature and in social community, can help to recall philosophers and others to the ongoing reality of our problematic situation and to their duty to contribute to cooperative social inquiry and communal reconstruction.

2

William James
and the Ethics of Fulfillment

To maintain that William James was essentially a moralist is hardly a controversial claim. Josiah Royce wrote that James was "profoundly ethical in his whole influence," and this viewpoint has been echoed over the years by commentators like R. B. Perry, John Wild, H. S. Thayer, and Abraham Edel. However, although the moral tone of James's thought has been recognized, his ethics has not been sufficiently explored. One reason for this is that James, as Royce noted, "really made very little of the formal office of an ethical teacher and seldom wrote upon technical ethical controversies."[1] Second, what ethical works of his there are reflect James's own lucid lecture style and hence seem to need little or no exploration. A third reason is the one I will stress here: the focus of James's ethical thought was on personal fulfillment, an area of ethics neglected in recent analysis. In the exploration of the moral thought of William James that follows, I hope to demonstrate the value of his ethical writings for helping us to understand more about ourselves, about our attempts at bettering human existence, and about the complex nature of morality itself.

In 1888–89, James offered an undergraduate course in moral philosophy at Harvard, the outline of which included the following analysis of good: "So far as I feel anything good, I make it so. It is so, for me. . . . *Prima facie,* goods form a multifarious jungle. . . . Of all the proposed *summa genera,* pleasure and perfection have the best claim to be considered. . . . these two standards do not conflict, but involve each other."[2] This small excerpt gives us in capsule form the thrust of his ethical position. Morality is a purely naturalistic matter. Elsewhere he writes in this same vein that "whether a God exist, or whether no God exist, in yon blue heaven above us bent, we form at any rate an ethical republic here below."[3] And the individual moral agent is James's focal point. Morality is not only naturalistic but also personal; pleasure and perfection involve each other.

Beyond this individualistic aspect of James's moral philosophy lies a social aspect that requires the creation of a better world so that individuals might live decently and happily. Now, admittedly, James was primarily a person for whom life itself is a wonderful mystery in which we should rejoice. Values were everywhere for James, and the only real sin was to live life without grasping its many glories. But this other aspect in his ethics is present as well, and it requires that individuals do what they can to better their world.

II

The first aspect of James's moral thought focuses upon personal fulfillment, the search for meanings and values. In our search, James cautions us, we are not to accept meanings and values secondhand or a priori. He writes in his diary on April 30, 1870, that "salvation" is not to be found in maxims. Over twenty years later, he reiterates that "there is no such thing possible as an ethical philosophy dogmatically made up in advance."[4] The reason for this fallibilism is that to set up any firm guidelines in advance would force all action, to be moral, into a predetermined mold. He remarks that this latter view was the deadening position of those who maintain that "there *must* be one system that is right and *every* other wrong." The inadequacy of this monism was clear to James: it is because of this narrow approach that we have had endless conflicts over which moral principle is the sole right one.[5] James admits that his moral theory, being a theory without any one answer, offers a world that some will see as "a dog without a collar." His emphasis is elsewhere, however, upon personal responsibility and the creation of individual values. In accordance with this personal focus he maintains that "there can be no final truth in ethics . . . until the last man has had his experience and said his say."[6]

People seek values and establish a system of meaning through their value choices. In our world of virtually unlimited possibilities, James writes, each of us must choose "what being he shall now resolve to become."[7] Because James was personally fascinated by the diverse ideals different individuals adopted, he was at the same time depressed by our normal inability to feel the values of others. From outside another person's life, he notes, we can seldom see the values that person sees. Even in his own case, he remarks, he was as blind to the particular ideals of the lives of some squatters "as they certainly would also have been to the ideality of mine, had they had a peep at my strange indoor academic ways of life at Cambridge."[8] This blindness is unfortunate in itself because it cuts us off from recognizing possible values. Perhaps more important, this blindness also leads to fear. Just as we fear what the unowned dog might do because the boundaries of its conduct are not as settled as those of a familiar dog, so too we fear the actions of those who have abandoned what one critic of James called "certain values transcending their particular interests of time and place"[9] for values of their own devising. We fear others because we do not see situations as they do and we do not know what they will take to be valuable.

This problem of fear arises from our involvement in our own worlds, the meaningfulness of which we have assembled and wish to preserve. We are not "philosophers but partisans," partisans for our own meanings. Each of us "is bound to feel intensely the importance of his own duties and the significance of the situations that call these forth." Our deadness toward the values of others is thus "the price we inevitably have to pay for being practical creatures."[10] Indeed, James believes that we would need to be virtually without any personal values at all before we could hope to gain a vital insight into the values of others. A concrete example of this blindness, James felt, was the bifurcation of society into owners and workers resulting from the fact that each segment of the population remains "entirely blind to the internal significance of the lives of the other half."[11] Such blindness is a direct result of our human partisanship, of the fact that we can see meaning and value in our lives only at the cost of not being able to appreciate the lives others lead.

The result of these considerations, James concludes, "absolutely forbids us to be forward in pronouncing on the meaninglessness of forms of existence other than our own; and it commands us to tolerate, respect, and indulge those whom we see harmlessly interested and happy in their own ways, however unintelligible these may be to us." If we cannot fully understand another's life, neither should we judge that person's conduct—just as we ourselves expect not to be judged. "Our inner secrets must remain for the most part impenetrable by others, for beings as essentially practical as we are are necessarily short of sight. But if we cannot gain much positive insight into one another, cannot we at least use our sense of our own blindness to make us more cautious in going over the dark places?" Each person should therefore "be faithful to his own opportunities and make the most of his own blessings, without presuming to regulate the rest of the vast field."[12] And thus we see that James's ethics is primarily an ethics of fulfillment.

III

In terms of reform and in choosing values for the group, James's position, as just outlined, would seem to be of no value, for he emphasizes being open to the possibilities of experience and allowing others the freedom to operate under their own lights. Still, his moral philosophy is not without an ethics of reform. This second aspect of James's ethical theory is not as pronounced in his writings, but it is surely there. In *Pragmatism*, for example, he reminds us, "The way of escape from evil . . . is *not* by getting it 'aufgehoben,' or preserved in the whole as an element essential but 'overcome.' *It is by dropping it out altogether, throwing it overboard and getting beyond it, helping to make a universe that shall forget its very place and name.*" In a moral situation, we must attempt to transform reality. We must decide and act, without such certainty as we would like, because moral questions present themselves "as questions whose solution cannot wait for sensible proof."[13] Morality requires action toward a world that will have forgotten the meaning of evil.

The question we must ask James here is how the group is to decide which are the evils that are to be thrown overboard and which are the goods that are to be saved. For individual persons, as we have seen, so far as they feel anything to be good, they *make* it good. But in a world of many people, in a moral pluriverse, the philosopher and ethical reformer tries to bring order by indicating some *desideranda* to which the mere *desiderata* should yield. James offered a method to choose among such ideals, but it is not a method of exclusion, that is, one holding that some *desiderata* are themselves less valuable than others. His method of value choice for society is a method of *inclusion, desideranda* being those goods that cut off the fewest possibilities of other goods. "The actually possible in this world is vastly narrower than all that is demanded," he writes, "and there is always a *pinch* between the ideal and the actual which can only be got through by leaving part of the ideal behind." In a world like this our "one unconditional commandment" is "that we should seek incessantly, with fear and trembling, so to vote and to act as to bring about the very largest total universe of good which we can see."[14] While in his early outline James admits that "the abstract best would be that *all* goods should be realized," he recognizes that we do not live in such a world. Ours is a world where choices must be made. "The whole difficulty of the moral life consists in deciding," he writes, "which goods to sacrifice and which to save."[15]

The reformist aspect of James's moral philosophy consists in the recognition that part of doing all that we can to make the individual's life worthwhile is the attempt to make the world a sufficiently better place so as to make fuller individual lives possible. This attempt involves making social choices. However, not all commentators believe that James's ethics of reform, because of its prior emphasis upon openness to individual possibilities and its method of inclusion, is sufficient to the task of moral leadership in our contemporary world. It is to these criticisms that we now turn.

IV

In a 1943 essay entitled "On a Certain Blindness in William James," Max C. Otto suggested that James's emphasis upon (what I am calling) the ethics of fulfillment left him unable to see the increasing need for an emphasis upon the ethics of reform in the modern world. In spite of his admiration for James's "uncanny aptness for catching the luster of a life wherever and however it was lived," Otto maintains that something equally important was being overlooked. James, he writes, "treated certain important social facts as he might have brushed against strangers in a crowd." Otto criticizes James on two grounds: his failure to recognize the long-term impact of inadequate living conditions upon children and adults, and his failure to appreciate workers' organized efforts to do something about their plight. He recognizes the importance of James's ethics of fulfillment but denies that such an ethics is adequate in the modern world.[16]

Otto does not base his criticism simply on the fact that James grew up serenely in the eye of the storm of industrialization—that he enjoyed "advantages."[17] Rather, Otto discounts the reformist aspect of James's ethical position because he believes that James's approach was essentially individualistic: "like Emerson, he was captivated by the ideal of absolutely unentangled and unfettered individuality."[18] An adequate ethics of reform, Otto maintains, requires a social basis. Other commentators have made similar points about James's individualism and his emphasis upon the ethics of fulfillment. Vivian J. McGill, for example, points to the incongruity of James's "withering attacks upon the Absolutes of Bradley and Royce" while having "nothing to say against the basic tyrannies and prejudices in the economic world." McGill believes that the latter "were surely more dangerous to the zest and rich variety of life [James] desired than the poor dragons of Bradley and Royce which he slew so gaily."[19] More recently, the relative unimportance of the ethics of reform for James has been clearly documented by George R. Garrison and Edward H. Madden. James, they note, was "not much of a reformer." He had "unexpected blind spots on the issues of racism, women's rights, British oppression of the Irish, and British imperialism in general." They too feel that it was James's individualism that "kept him from acting in concern with others through effective organizations to bring to bear cumulative pressure."[20]

The question here is not whether James was cold toward the suffering of others, for he was not.[21] Even granting his recognition of the severe social and economic problems of his society, however, his individualistic tone and method of inclusion do not seem to offer us any help in our attempts to address these social ills as they appear in our world. Although James believed, for example, that the maldistribution of wealth was changing in favor of some new socialistic equilibrium, he did not see this resolution as a higher social condition for which we should strive. Moreover, he writes that, should we expect that these eventual changes will make "any *genuine vital difference* on a large scale," we will have missed what he felt makes a life significant.[22]

James did not think that the workers' unhappy lives were simply the result of economic conditions; consequently he did not believe that even radical changes in these conditions were likely to give them meaning. "The barrenness and ignobleness of the more usual laborer's life consist in the fact that it is moved by no . . . ideal inner springs," James writes. "The backache, the long hours, the danger, are patiently endured—for what? To gain a quid of tobacco, a glass of beer, a cup of coffee, a meal, and a bed, and to begin again the next day and shirk as much as one can." The workers in society were living solely to stay alive—which was, for James, somehow ignoble in itself. To be noble, he writes, a life must be lived in accord with "some inner *ideal*."[23] However, adding somewhat to Otto, surely James would have said in a clearer moment that these workers lived in accordance with an ideal—an ideal that he, as a partisan of his own values, could not understand. Thus James, in an open violation of his own position, seems to have felt that the workers' values—whatever they were—were not to be considered. Far more serious still for Otto was James's apparent inability to recognize the important role played by economic security as at least a prerequisite to a worthwhile life. Before an inner ideal can be of use to a person, Otto believes, that person must enjoy at least some minimal level of social welfare.

Otto thus points specifically to James's failure to understand the role of social institutions, particularly economic ones, in modern life. For James, he writes, "social institutions endangered the purity of individuality. Even organizations formed to combat economic injustice . . . were likely . . . to be a greater evil than the evil they were intended to remedy." As James himself puts it, "The bigger the unit you deal with, the hollower, the more brutal, the more mendacious is the life displayed."[24] In his defense of personal value, James's individualism thus *opposes institutions as obstacles* rather than *uses them as means* to the fulfillment of individuality. He cannot emphasize the need for social reconstruction of our institutions as a means to fuller lives because the institutions themselves, reconstructed or not, are deadening. The ethics of fulfillment, at least in his formulation, is in a fundamental way opposed to the ethics of reform. Moreover, there is nowhere in James's writings the sense that individualism itself could lead to social problems; or diversity, to anarchy. For him, human atavisms are fostered in groups, as indicated in his discussions of jingoism and lynching. When individuals become part of something external to themselves—whether a political party, a lynch mob, or a country—this ideality is abandoned. However, when individuals choose values in an intelligent and responsible fashion and shape their lives around these vibrant values, social good results. All we need to make this possible, Arthur E. Murphy notes dryly, is "a world of individuals as genial and generous as William James."[25]

Otto suggests that an important reason for James's blindness is that "the time had not come—for most people it has not yet come—to recognize the vital interdependence of the individual and the environmental objects and procedures by means of which he lives and achieves. This truth was still to be elucidated by John Dewey."[26] Consequently, James could still—as Dewey later could no longer—focus upon the importance of the individual considered apart from the group and the socioeconomic factors of life and emphasize the primacy of the ethics of fulfillment. The need that James felt to protect the individual from the external was not translatable—as it was in Dewey—into a need to unite in group self-protection against economic and other forces too strong for individuals to deal with in isolation. James's ethics of fulfillment is not translatable into an ethics of reform, and consequently, as Merle E. Curti writes, James's position was "incompatible with the full development of the very individuality of the masses of Americans for which in principle James sincerely stood."[27]

V

A fuller comparison between James and Dewey will be helpful at this point because they offer radically different positions within the same dual framework of the ethics of fulfillment and the ethics of reform. In his *Art as Experience* (LW 10), for example, Dewey points to the importance of recognizing the meanings in all experience. His emphasis in most of his other works, however, is on helping to solve social prob-

lems through institutional reconstruction. The primary ethical difference between James and Dewey is thus not that they hold contradictory
positions on particular ethical issues or even on theoretical principles.
It is rather that Dewey, along with the other Pragmatic social thinkers,
emphasizes the social aspect to the downplaying of the individual,
whereas James's emphasis is just the reverse.

To explore this difference in emphasis further, I wish to draw out
some differences between James and Dewey on two specific points: first,
why the sort of good life that James seeks cannot be obtained through
Dewey's position; second, how the means that James proposes we use
to reach his ethical ideal lead him away from Dewey's position. Considering first James's ideal of the good life, we see that for him there
is, initially at least, an emptiness in human existence. Meaning must be
created by people—both Dewey and James would espouse this position.
But James wants more meaning, and meaning of a different sort, than
Dewey can offer. In particular, as John E. Smith writes, James wants
"a higher power which can complete life and overcome the destructive
forces in it."[28] James understands this power to be a God who can
guarantee "an ideal order that shall be permanently preserved," a guarantee that Dewey neither would seek nor could accept. It is also true
that James believes that "our responsibility ends with the performance
of [our] duty, and the burden of the rest we may lay on higher powers,"[29]
the existence of which Dewey would unquestionably deny. James clearly
wants a supernatural realm to add extra meaning to that which we
fashion in this world. Consequently he can write that materialism—in
Dewey's or any other formulation—"means simply the denial that the
moral order is eternal, and the cutting off of ultimate hopes; spiritualism
means the affirmation of an eternal moral order and the letting loose
of hope." Dewey would admit that his materialism denied any "ultimate
hopes" and the possibility of the eternality of the moral order; but, for
him, this denial is a prerequisite for the reconstruction of our ethical
systems. "We and God have business with each other," writes James.[30]
Dewey on this point would no doubt say that the peoples of the earth
have business with each other, not with God, and this business is to
work toward the acceptance of values under which we can live together
as a community.

James was attempting to regain old values that science and materialism had taken away. He was still attempting to answer the old questions
in a world that was increasingly meeting new problems that gave rise
to questions of a different sort. Dewey no longer anguished over the
existence of a God, nor over freedom and determinism, the reality of
morality, or the proofs of immortality. Those questions—in James's

terms—were not "live" for Dewey. For Dewey, and the other Social
Pragmatists, we are increasingly "at home" in the world.[31] Although
Dewey's naturalism offers none of the grandeur of the supernaturalism
that James seeks, it has the advantage of not needing to salve the anguish
that precipitated James's search. Dewey's naturalism addresses new
questions, such as the following:

—Where are we, as a society, going?
—What future do we wish to build for ourselves and for our children?
—How can the members of our society and the peoples of the world
get along with each other?
—How should the bounty of the earth be managed?

These are the questions of Dewey's good life, as distinct from James's.
They are social questions, questions for the ethics of reform.

A second difference between James and Dewey has to do with the
means each suggests to reach the moral ideal. And here we see that
James's means for achieving his good life lead him away from the position that Pragmatic social thought was to affirm. Because these new
questions are social questions, the answers to them must be developed
through social interaction and group choice. To do this, we need a
method of criticism, and the search for such a method of criticism turns
us away from James and his noncritical openness toward Dewey. We
recall that James wants a significant life in a pluralistic universe. Individuals must make this significance for themselves by living in accord
with a vital ideal. A correlative to this requirement is that each individual's values, provided they do not "interfere by violence with ours,"[32]
are somehow sacrosanct. Consequently, short of an indefensible reinterpretation of the meaning of the term *violence*, James's approach does
not offer us a framework to seek values to undergird a social reform
movement when our problem is a lack of sufficient resources for all to
live as they might see fit. Criticism is an essential part of modern social
life, and on occasion we must reject some individuals' values.

It is on this matter of the criticism of values, which James eschewed,
that I see his position to be inadequate to the modern situation, and it
is because of this lack of a critical stance that I relegate his ethics of
fulfillment to a secondary position. To be desired is not necessarily to
be valuable, especially in a world of artificially inflated wants. We cannot
simply, as James would have us, "follow the windings of the spectacle,
confident that the line of least resistance will always be towards the
richer and the more inclusive arrangement, and that by one tack after
another some approach to the kingdom of heaven is incessantly made."[33]

We have neither the guarantees nor the resultant optimism that James had. We must seek the best and least costly way to perform the tasks that have to be done; we cannot simply adopt the option that enables us to perform the greatest variety of tasks. To criticize, in this sense, it is necessary to relegate certain goods to lesser roles and to close our eyes to the lesser beauties of nature. The social aspect of Dewey's method allows for attempts at critical reconstruction of our environment to facilitate the development of fuller lives for individuals. James's position in general, with its individualistic tone and its method of inclusion, unfortunately does not allow for this type of reconstruction. His primary emphasis upon the understanding of the ethics of fulfillment prevents the development of an ethics of reform.

VI

Although James's moral thought largely undercuts the possibility of social reconstruction, his discussion of war as a social problem is happily another story. He offers, in "The Moral Equivalent of War," an essay published in 1910, a clear indication of his recognition that the military situation in the modern world was not amenable to individual control. Too much military power had accumulated in the hands of those who benefited from its use, and a reconstruction of the whole military complex and its role in our society was necessary before we could hope to establish pacifism as a viable position. James ridicules those who maintain that war is the result of divine will and those for whom expansion is the only alternative to decay. And he clearly indicates the extent to which research and development activities are actually the wars of tomorrow fought today in the laboratory and the supply room: " 'peace' and 'war' mean the same thing, now *in posse,* now *in actu.* . . . the intensely sharp competitive *preparation* for war by the nations is the *real war.* . . . the battles are only a sort of public verification of the military mastery gained during the 'peace'-interval."[34] He also cut through the cant of the generals and others for whom a war is always defensive and always reluctantly accepted only after all other possibilities have been repudiated by the other side.

Because James recognizes that condemnation of the evils related to war is not enough, he maintains that only after our society is significantly reconstructed will we be able to adopt a new stance. "The military feelings are too deeply grounded to abdicate their place among our ideals until better substitutes are offered," he writes. Consequently pacifists need "to enter more deeply into the esthetical and ethical point of view of their opponents." Otherwise, he continues, they will never be able to understand the values that militarists have associated with the military life—values that might be preserved through a better social organization without the military aspects of our present system. "Martial virtues must be the enduring cement; intrepidity, contempt of softness, surrender of private interest, obedience to command, must still remain the rock upon which states are built—unless, indeed, we wish for dangerous reactions against commonwealths fit only for contempt, and liable to invite attack whenever a centre of crystallization for military-minded enterprise is formed anywhere in their neighborhood." War functions in our society, James writes, as "a sort of sacrament" that is believed to keep society healthy and strong.[35] Consequently it will remain indispensable until we develop our social intelligence to a level at which it is capable of effecting adequate organization. This reorganization is necessary because no society can be expected to abandon war until it feels that it has another way to instill the values that militarism now brings.

James thus maintains that we must rescue patriotism from the militarists—a task that he does not believe will be easy. "The war against war," he writes, "is going to be no holiday excursion or camping party." Besides our need for a social focus of our affections, a need that can be manipulated by the media, by government, and by others, we are also a belligerent lot. "Our ancestors have bred pugnacity into our bone and marrow, and thousands of years of peace won't breed it out of us." To make use of the values of the military life and to sublimate some of this pugnacity, he proposes a conscription of all the young to serve in the war against nature. (Today we would no doubt rephrase this "in the war to *save* nature.") "Hardihood" and "discipline" would be developed in our young, and the country would be better off for it. James believes that what he called the "martial type of character" was itself desirable; and, once divorced from the militarist consciousness, it could be "bred without war."[36]

In his discussion of the problem of war, James clearly understands the importance of the social structure and group psychology to the ethical realm. He indicates that an important prerequisite of living a good life is first making the world a better place—a place where the people turn the positive values of the martial spirit against the true enemies of humankind and not against each other. However, James still misses the extent to which an individual country within a system of rival nation states cannot commit itself to pacifism in isolation from the activities of its fellows. It is thus that the individualistic tone of his moral thought ultimately works against him here also. Perhaps in 1910 the oceans seemed wide enough for isolated pacifism. Events shortly thereafter proved they were not, and James's notion of a moral equivalent of war was abandoned for the headier moral potions of Woodrow Wilson and others. James was right that a person cannot be a practical pacifist in a militarist country, but he overlooked the fact that neither can a country be pacifist unless the world itself is at peace.[37]

VII

We have examined James's ethics as primarily an ethics of fulfillment, an ethics that places little emphasis upon criticism and evaluation and much emphasis upon the importance of openness to the ways in which others understand experience. Of these two aspects of a moral approach, we often take the ethics of reform, the ethics of change and of social reconstruction, to be primary at our moment in the twentieth century. I have done so myself in declaring it a weakness of James's ethics that he emphasizes the ethics of fulfillment over the ethics of reform. I will attempt to demonstrate throughout the rest of this volume why I believe the ethics of reform must be primary. In closing this consideration of James, however, I would like to suggest the necessity for the continued recognition of an ethics of fulfillment.

We emphasize the present injustices of living, as we must. We lament the past sufferings of humankind as unnecessary. We cry out for a future when equality would prevail. Yet we know that sufferings will never end, that neither justice nor equality will ever completely triumph. We say with Dewey, "Nothing but the best, the richest and fullest experience possible, is good enough" for humankind (LW 1:308). Yet all the while we know that experience seldom matches up to even our most limited expectations. To base our ethics on attempts at bettering the world is to assume something like the task of Sisyphus.

Some, like Dewey, *are able to* assume this task and assume it cheerfully: "Does not this reduce moral life to the futile toil of a Sisyphus who is forever rolling a stone uphill only to have it roll back so that he has to repeat his old task? Yes, judged from progress made in a control of conditions which shall stay put and which excludes the necessity of future deliberations and reconsiderations."[38] Not all can be so staunch in the face of futility, however meaningful to others, and there are those who fully expect the rock to stay up there, at least one of these days, at least for a short while. Otherwise, pushing it can only be seen as a waste of effort. Such people look forward to the "moral holidays"[39] that would then occur. In this regard, James cited Emerson's early position on the slavery question: " 'God must govern his own world, and knows his way out of this pit without my desertion of my post, which has none to guard it but me. I have quite other slaves to face than those negroes, to wit, imprisoned thoughts far back in the brain of man, and which have no watchman or lover or defender but me.' "[40]

Moral thinkers like Emerson and James emphasize the ethics of fulfillment. Value is everywhere. Life is for rejoicing. Let each person find worth wherever possible. Judge no one and impose no values on others. This emphasis is *not just a weakness* in their moral philosophy; rather, it is an emphasis upon an aspect of moral life that we now tend, rightly I would maintain, to discount. However, as James correctly indicates, social justice is neither an absolute prerequisite for, nor a certain guarantee of, individual fulfillment. Social reform, and hence the ethics of reform, is not itself enough either for a society to be moral or for its citizens to be fulfilled. It is necessary to keep in mind that both the ethics of fulfillment and the ethics of reform are necessary for an adequate moral philosophy.

3

George Herbert Mead on
Intelligent Social Reconstruction

George Herbert Mead once wrote that we are no longer "pilgrims and strangers" in the world. "We are at home in our own world" because it is a world that has come to us not "by inheritance but by conquest." Unlike a world that comes down to us from the past and thereby "possesses and controls us," we can possess and control our world since it is one that we "discover and invent." All in all, he writes, this new life of mastery amounts to "a splendid adventure if we can rise to it" (SW 266). Mead was far from alone in the belief that the twentieth century had possibilities that were markedly greater than those that had ever existed previously. In the words of Walter Lippmann, it had become possible "to substitute purpose for tradition."[1] Another of the major proponents of deliberate collective action, John Dewey, wrote that it was now "possible for human beings to take hold of human affairs and manage them, to see an end which has to be gained, a purpose which must be fulfilled, and deliberately and intelligently to go to work to organize the means, the resources and the methods of accomplishing those results" (MW 11:82). It is perhaps most telling for our troubled century that Dewey's discussion referred specifically not to advances in health care or in providing for the nutritional needs of the world's burgeoning population. Rather, he was describing our recently achieved ability to organize our total social lives to defeat our opponents in the First World War.

Most of Mead's contemporaries seemed to have agreed with him that intelligent social action had become attainable, but many were less sanguine about our possibilities. Those who disagreed assumed that it was impossible to effect intelligent change by means of existing social and political institutions. To some, this view meant that no democratic government could be expected to act intelligently. One such critic, H. L. Mencken, saw democracy as a symbiotic, if ultimately self-destructive, relationship between the grasping mob and a series of rival demagogues who were willing to barter the long-term social good for votes. Mencken did not anticipate a long future for democracy—being fairly certain that it was "a self-limiting disease"—but, in the meantime, it captivated his attention because it was so "incomparably idiotic, and hence incomparably amusing."[2] For some other critics, among them Edward Lee Thorndike, the ultimate futility of popular democracy was just as real, if less amusing. The conduct of our affairs must be willingly ceded by the technically incompetent average citizens to the experts, Thorndike tells us, since "the issues of the twentieth century are too complex and difficult to be played with by amateurs. The general common sense that was admirable for the tasks of the town meeting of our fathers is hopelessly inadequate for the municipal problems of to-day." Because these average individuals are intellectually unable to address our present ills, he continues, to call for broadening the popular method of political action is to call for greater manipulation of the masses, who will always remain "easy prey to the selfishness of politicians, the seductiveness of salesmen, and the enthusiasm of fanatics."[3] For both of these critics, and for many others, we could not hope to act intelligently in our social affairs as long as our social decisions continued to be made in accordance with existing democratic procedures.

Another line of attack on the possibility of intelligent social action suggests that the weakness of our democracy is that our social decisions never have been made in accordance with true democratic procedures. Although critics of this sort often disagree about the means of remedying our situation, they agree that no capitalist parliamentary democracy could be expected to act in the interests of the general populace. In the words of one such critic, William Zebulon Foster, "the capitalist democracy is a sham" in which voting and other democratic institutions "are only so many screens to hide the capitalist autocracy and to make it more palatable to the masses." Therefore, we cannot expect our governmental machinery to address the needs of the vast majority of the residents of our society unless these needs correspond directly with those of the monied few. The members of this economic and political elite, Foster notes, "will never voluntarily give up control of society and abdicate their system of exploiting the masses," and they cannot be "talked, bought, or voted out of power." In Foster's eyes, short of the necessary revolution and the creation of a Soviet America, our society could not hope to ever intelligently address its social problems.[4]

Still others suggest that, even if all our citizens cooperated in attempts to advance the common good, "things" are just too complicated in the modern world to allow for intelligent social action: "things" move too fast; "things" are too interrelated, too complex; "things" (to hearken back to Emerson) "are in the saddle, / And ride mankind."[5] In the minds of adherents to this perspective, pace Thorndike, even the technique of our most intelligent leaders cannot save us. One of the most articulate holders of this position, Joseph Wood Krutch, put it this way: "man's ingenuity has outrun his intelligence. He was good enough to survive in a simple, sparsely populated world, where he was neither powerful enough nor in sufficiently close contact with his neighbors to do them or himself fatal harm. He is not good enough to manage the more complicated and closely integrated world which he is, for the first time, powerful enough to destroy." The truly wise, Krutch believed, rather than counting on intelligent collective action leading to social "evolution" anticipate "catastrophe."[6] Although we have managed to stave off this anticipated catastrophe for decades, its possibility is just as real as ever. To disagree with Mencken, however idiotic the modern world may seem to some, it is not "amusing."

Is intelligent social action possible? If it is, under what social setting will it be achieved most effectively? These two questions are of supreme importance in our modern world; yet they are questions with many conflicting answers. But before considering these questions, I would like to take up a related but logically prior question in the hope of clearing up some of the difficulties surrounding these two. That is, what would intelligent social action be? Let us explore this topic through an examination of the Pragmatic social thought of George Herbert Mead.

II

Initially, Mead's work might not seem to be a particularly auspicious place to begin exploring the possibilities of intelligent social action. This is so even though everyone familiar with his work recognizes that Mead possessed a remarkably original mind. Many of us would be happy to admit, with Dewey, that our own thought would have been greatly impoverished "were it not for the seminal ideas which [we] derived from him" (LW 6:24). But most philosophers, and even many philosophers with a deep interest in American thought, see Mead as meriting only tangential treatment and as having little to say on questions of collective social action.[7]

One explanation of this mistaken evaluation of Mead's work is that most readers, it seems, come to his work through *Mind, Self, and Society,* his most striking—and most difficult—contribution. Because of the powerful impact of the "I" and the "me," of the "emergent self" and the "Generalized Other," these readers overemphasize the importance of this volume in Mead's corpus. As a result, his social psychology functions not as a liberating perspective that lays open new possibilities in his other works but as a set of restrictive blinders on those readers who approach them. Indeed, *Mind, Self, and Society* is such a difficult book that many readers go no further. Their general impression of what Mead's work is about, based upon an insufficient exploration of that work, is what leads them to suppose that Mead might not have much to say about intelligent social action. In fact, Mead has a great deal to say, if we approach his work in the proper manner.

My suggestion is to examine his work from the point of view of reconstruction,[8] an approach that will open up his thought for the larger tasks of Pragmatic social thought. For Mead, all nature addresses and solves problems; all nature—but especially the living organism—reconstructs. "Life is a process of continued reconstruction," he tells us. Lest we underplay the significance he wishes to place in this continuum of reconstruction, he continues: "The animal is doing the same thing the scientist is doing. It is facing a problem, selecting some element in the situation which may enable it to carry its act through to completion" (MT 292, 346). Both are addressing a problem and attempting a solution through reconstruction.

Reconstruction, Mead tells us, takes place on three levels: the physical or chemical, the biological, and the intelligent. I wish to focus upon the latter two levels, stressing the importance of what Dewey calls "the naturalization of intelligence" (LW 4:156–77). "It would be a mistake," Mead notes, to assume that a person is a "biologic individual plus a reason, if we mean by this definition that he leads two separable lives, one of impulse or instinct, and another of reason" (MSS 347). When properly understood, knowing is "as natural a process as running or eating or bearing children, as living or dying."[9] Thinking and knowing are the actions of a live and involved creature. In spite of our involvement in our own thinking and knowing, and even to some extent because of it, Mead maintains, it is possible to think clearly and objectively. Because we are vitally concerned with the results of our actions, our thinking and knowing must be as objective as possible and remain open to experience and change.

A close examination of thinking indicates, as we have just seen, the implication of the whole person in our purposive activities. As Dewey refers to the reflex arc as a "single concrete whole" (EW 5:97), Mead tells us that "the unit of existence in human experience is the act, within which nothing is there that does not involve successive phases" (PA 66). Mead's approach is admittedly a behaviorism; but his *social* behaviorism offers us, he believes, "an approach to the study of the experience of the individual from the point of view of his conduct, particularly, but not exclusively, the conduct as it is observable by others" (MSS 2). The individual approaches particular actional situations with attitudinal preconditions that Mead recognizes to be "the beginnings of acts" (MSS 5). For example, when we approach a tool with which we are familiar, we will be prepared to grasp the tool properly, to use it safely and productively, and to maintain its long-term usefulness.

Oftentimes in living there develops what Mead describes as "a lack of adjustment between the individual and his world" (PA 6). This problem gives rise to emotional discomfort and random action and, in humans, to thought. In Mead's terms, the individual is shocked from "the attitude of immediate experience" to the attitude of "reflective analysis" (PA 14), that is, from operating on a kind of prereflective automatic pilot to a conscious examining of the problem. For recurring problems we develop habits that actually become incorporated into our central nervous systems. And, although "one may respond to well-recognized cues by well-formed habits," one can also "adapt and reconstruct his habits by new interpretation of the situation" (SW 90). This conscious intellectual reconstruction is possible, Mead writes, because of our ability to interrupt the flow of action and to expand the situation by means of the significant symbols made available by speech. In this way, it is possible to search for a possible solution—for a hypothesis that can be tested first in thought and then in action.

Even Mead's social behaviorism is too behavioristic for some, and critics of his work have felt that his naturalizing of thought has denied crucial aspects of thinking. We may not want to follow him all the way to the claim that "reasoning conduct appears where impulsive conduct breaks down" or to the position that "in reflective intelligence one thinks to act. . . . Thinking becomes preparatory to social action" (MSS 348, 141). Similarly, we may not share what Kenneth Burke has called Mead's "Whitmanesque delight" in facing situation after situation "wherein each solution is the basis of a new problem,"[10] as in Mead's rhetorical question, "Is not life a continuous solution of problems?" (SW 331). But we clearly do see that Mead is offering us a powerful way to think about our lives, a way that is as applicable to science, history, and medicine as it is to literature, philosophy, and dance. Because he sees reconstruction as the fundamental model of human action, his work offers us a perspective from which we might rethink our analysis of social action.

III

Although, for Mead, as we have just seen, to be human is to be reconstructive, this reconstruction can be done in a better or worse fashion—
a distinction that Dewey compares to the one "between good and bad
farming or good and bad medical practice" (LW 12:107). Considering
Mead's model of human action as reconstructive, what are the possibilities for intelligent social reconstruction? Especially if we take as seriously as he does the importance of habit and unplanned action in
human life, to what degree can we expect appropriateness of response
in our collective action? And, even though an implicated stance may be
better than a detached and olympian stance for the *recognition* of problems, how can these radically natural creatures *address* such problems
intelligently? How likely *is* intelligent social action among creatures such
as we?

Perhaps the way to initially approach this question is to examine
Mead's understanding of intelligence. On the broadest level, Mead uses
the term *intelligence* to describe any mode of response by an organism
that "maintains or advances the interests of the form or the species to
which it belongs" (MSS 328). This post factum analysis of intelligence—
which could be used to describe the successful actions of a plant, for
example (see MT 345)—gives way to a more focused analysis of intelligence that relates it to the conscious foresight of consequences. Intelligence in this narrower sense refers to our power to present to
ourselves "what is going to happen," to anticipate the future "in terms
of ideas" (MSS 119). Intelligence thus gives us the possibility of thinking
through, rather than acting out, suggested solutions. Here the examples
from Dewey, mentioned above, can be considered. The distinction between simply lucky farming or medicine and their intelligent counter-
parts is minimally that the latter processes make conscious use of good
and bad past fortune to influence future actions. "Action that employs
the past," Mead tells us, "in reducing [the] uncertainty from the standpoint of the result toward which the act moves, we call 'intelligent' in
the most general sense of that word" (PA 68).

Intelligent reconstruction thus looks to both the direct and indirect
consequences of our attempts at mastery. In terms of a global problem
like overpopulation, for example, the intelligent approach would be to
examine the consequences of our specific actions upon the many facets
of the problem including the many indirect results of our actions, as
well as the costs of any particular strategy versus alternative strategies
that were not undertaken. In addition, we also need to seek out new
problems, as well as the undiscovered aspects of current ones, so that

we can be continuously ready to readjust to new developments. Finally, we must work as if success is possible. These corollaries to Mead's Pragmatic view require closer examination.

Intelligent social action must seek out new problems and unexamined aspects of currently recognized problems. Familiar as we are with the more or less continuous series of problems in living, we recognize that we do not address all of them in a self-conscious fashion. And, although initially satisfactory solutions oftentimes take place "far below the threshold of reflective experience" (PA 504), we recognize the long-term inadequacy of these haphazard methods. Moreover, Peirce's reminder of the extent to which beliefs can be fixed in an inadequate fashion so as to merely quiet doubt, as well as James's assertion that the sentiment of rationality is itself just "the absence of any feeling of irrationality," should help to remind us of the extent to which our problems can be, and have been, avoided rather than addressed.[11] All too often we have been satisfied just to end *the feeling of the problem* rather than to address the problem itself. Therefore, unless we assume from the start that all our problems will ultimately solve themselves, we need to make a conscious and deliberate effort to seek them out and anticipate and preclude their most damaging consequences.

This is a lesson we have been slow to learn. For example, we are only now beginning to address overpopulation in an intelligent manner. Another example is our failure to recognize until very recently the complex environmental problems facing us. Moreover, these two increasingly emphasized problems are not the only ones confronting us—and they may not even be the most serious ones. With this warning ever in mind, we should recognize the important role individuals play in bringing to light ills not yet commonly recognized. Mead tells us that "problems can appear only in the experience of the individual" (MT 411); unless individuals are able to bring to social consciousness anticipated ills, we will never be able to respond to them. All in all, then, to intelligently address social problems we need to strive to make reflective reconstruction a greater part of our total actions by seeking after problems, being especially careful to listen to the reports of individuals.

Secondly, intelligent social action should also abandon any hope for ultimate solutions and instead adopt a model of continual readjustment. "Things emerge," Mead tells us, "which could not be predicted from what has happened before" (PA 88), and consequently the process of intelligent action must be "one of conduct which is continually adjusting itself to new situations" (MT 290). To act otherwise is to confuse a plan that should be developing through interaction with the situation with "a creed" to be followed or "a program" that has been worked out in advance and needs only to be enacted.[12] Therefore, all of our social actions, to be intelligent, should also be cast in the form of a "working hypothesis" (SW 3), which is to be tested and modified in action.

The openness that we have examined in the first corollary would be of little use without the commitment found in the second corollary, which is that we must modify our plans to make use of these new insights. Similarly, the emphasis upon testing and modification in this second corollary would make no sense unless success were a possibility. A third lesson, then, is that intelligent social action should assume that at least some level of success is possible. The position of Pragmatic social thought on the question of optimism and social faith (see chapter 7), is simply that social action is likely to be effective only when it is carried out with some hope that it might succeed. This is not to endorse the foolhardy delusion that success is a certainty. To cite just two reasons why success cannot be so guaranteed, I need only mention the importance of emergent conditions and the indispensability of sensitive individuals in pointing out impending evils. Moreover, because we have to act in social situations, "however inadequate our plan of action may be" (SW 257), we often cannot wait for satisfactory assurance of success. Yet this lack of guarantees ought not to suggest futility.

We need to focus on the fluidity in our situations—the same lack of determinateness that led to the development of our current imbalances and problems—and recognize that something can be done. Examining and modifying modes of action *can* lead to the solution of our ills. If we seek out problems before they come upon us full blown, and if we remain flexible in our modes of response, we will have a better chance at success. This emphasis upon believing in the possibility of success is, again, not the simple-minded delusion that solutions are certain or easy. Rather, it is a morale or a faith that recognizes that hope is a necessary prerequisite to dedicated effort. As such, Mead has had predecessors—James, for example, who writes that "faith is synonymous with working hypothesis." We cannot continue on with life without some level of faith in an unproven future.[13] The better world that we are seeking, Mead writes, "grows out of this world" (SW 404), and this better world is more likely to be achieved through deliberate social attempts to bring it about rather than through happenstance and whimsy or the blind following of a preset course of action.

Many excessive claims have been made about intelligence, but Mead's analysis does not require that we make them. If we can rise above the limitations of our habitual nature to a level of inquiring anticipation and turn from a focus upon elaborate and unbending solutions to those that we can more easily modify and adjust, if we believe in the possibility of success and address "the problems of present behavior in terms of its possible future consequences as implicated on the basis of past experience" (MSS 100)—then, Mead believes, we have the means to conduct ourselves more intelligently in our social actions.

IV

However sympathetic one might be with Mead's position thus far, his central suggestion that we look to the consequences of our actions needs to be examined further. Some mention ought to be made of particular consequences themselves and of the methods by which they are to be deemed acceptable. Consider, for example, overpopulation as a social problem. What would be an intelligent attempt to deal with it? Leaving aside absurd answers like the conquest and enslavement of so-called lesser peoples for the good of our own population, and avoiding other approaches such as genocide, infanticide, and enforced euthanasia, we still encounter major differences of opinion over the moral legitimacy of means like contraception and sterilization. Both of these approaches to controlling overpopulation, rooted in a sense of what is an intelligent response to a severe problem, have met with frequent and powerful opposition from those who see such measures as the triumph of convenience over morality or as a calculated attempt to selectively limit the population growth of certain groups to the advantage of others.

Perhaps more troubling than these disagreements are the suggestions of those who, having examined the anticipated consequences of our many options to control overpopulation, maintain that the "intelligent" thing to do, in effect, is to allow great numbers of people to starve to death rather than to feed them—lest they be able to reproduce and at some future point overtax our already straining lifeboat. It becomes apparent that, however closely we might follow Mead's analysis of the intelligent seeking of desirable future consequences, unanimous agreement as to what sorts of consequences should be deemed acceptable is unlikely.

As an example of how values might differ, we can examine briefly three particular social values that Mead advocates and compare them to values held by others. Mead, for example, would have us end the control of party politicians over municipal affairs. Mead believes that, although it might seem to some individuals that a party machine is the most successful way to achieve their favored political consequences, it does not operate for the long-term good of the whole community. Rather, in "the chasm that separates the theory and practice of our democracy" (SW 263), we find the self-aggrandizing party politician "who finds in the human situation his stock-in-trade."[14] On a broader scale, Mead also would have us put an end to competitive private-property capitalism and replace it with a largely socialistic mixed economy, one closer in spirit to the cooperative unit that our highly interrelated society implies but has not yet made possible. Here too his belief is that, in the long-run, the capitalist form of economic organization does not provide the best results. Third, to return to the local level, with regard to settlement houses Mead believes that social settlements approach community problems "with no preconceptions," without "dogma or fixed rules of conduct." Rather, as a part of the community, they seek to find out what the community's problems are and "help toward their solution."[15] For Mead, the fostering of social settlements, the adoption of a mixed economy, and the elimination of party politics would be intelligent modes of social action because they foster valuable social ends.

Others disagree over whether a thorough examination of social conditions should commit us to these actions or to alternative actions. For example, while Thorstein Veblen admitted that the work of the social settlement was "in part directed to enhance the industrial efficiency of the poor and to teach them the more adequate utilization of the means at hand," he also maintained that it was "no less consistently directed to the inculcation, by precept and example, of certain punctilios of upper-class propriety in manners and customs."[16] Similarly, there are those for whom a largely unfettered capitalism operating in the context of a 'free market' is the only just and moral—and, equally important, the only successful—way to run an economic system. As Herbert Hoover writes, "The penetration of Socialist methods even to a partial degree will demoralize the economic system, the legislative bodies, and in fact the whole system of ordered Liberty."[17] Last, there are those who advocate party politics as the only practical way for a political system to reflect the needs and desires of particular individuals adequately rather than the whims of a distant and unfeeling city hall.[18]

To the extent that these disagreements are related to objectively verifiable facts—facts that Mead would call "scientific"—further experiences would seem of necessity to lead to eventual social agreement. In this regard he rejects the bifurcation of science and values and suggests that we can derive values scientifically. It is mistaken, Mead writes, "to assume that scientific method is applicable only in the fashioning and selection of means, and may not be used where the problem involves conflicting social ends or values" (SW 254). Presumably then, with dedicated work—with work that was undertaken intelligently, in the sense described above—eventually we could attain agreement upon a broad set of common values that we could then promote through our social actions.

Even so, Mead himself admits that the evidence for any such convergence is as yet inconclusive. "We have never been so uncertain," he maintains, "as to what are the values which economics undertakes to define, what are the political rights and obligations of citizens" (PP 167), to cite just two cases. Moreover, there is Mead's own admission during World War I that no individual who disagrees with the majority's evaluation should be punished "for acting in accordance with the dictates of one's own moral judgment."[19] This statement indicates that he expects such disagreements to continue in the future. If they do continue—as it seems they must—then perhaps we will have to admit that these different evaluations of human goods are not related to factual disputes but stem from different positions on the nature of a good human life. In terms of Mead's own reconstructive analysis of human nature, this ongoing diversity can be explained by remembering that problems are recognized as felt needs by certain individuals based upon their vision of what an adequate human life is. But, as we have seen with the problem of the world's growing population, this admission means that Mead's belief that "the problem itself defines the values" (MSS 388) is correct only to the extent that the problem itself is agreed upon already. One way to achieve this prior agreement is through the fostering of collective values in a community, and this is the method that Mead adopts.

V

In examining the role that Mead believes the community must play in intelligent social action, we see that its importance is central. It is by means of the community that goods are evaluated. The role of the community in Mead's work is also a more subtle one than is often recognized. Although Mead may believe, as Paul E. Pfuetze suggests, that "education, socialization, and the cultivation of free critical inquiry are all that is needed to set men on the path toward socially valuable goals,"[20] Mead would not suggest that our current substitutes for education, socialization, and free inquiry are likely to have the same effect. Mead distinguishes clearly between "social" and "moral"—that is, between those social actions "which give rise to friendly attitudes and relations, and those which give rise to hostile attitudes and relations, among the human individuals implicated in the social situations." Still, Mead believes that any far-reaching reconstruction of society "presupposes a basis of common social interests shared by all the individual members of the given human society in which that reconstruction occurs" (MSS 304, 308).

He believes as well that the modern interrelated and interdependent world has created a social good. This belief is reflected in what he feels is an expanding recognition of our interdependent public welfare that includes art, health care, public security, better housing conditions, more adequate schooling, playgrounds and parks, community and social centers, and so on (cf. PA 497; SW 234). In fact, Mead tells us that the level of civilization itself is to be found "in the intelligence and will of the community in making these common interests the means and the reason for converting diversities into social organization" (SW 366). However, he also recognizes that this realization of social interdependence had not yet been converted into the creation of a common good—that is, a good that benefits all in a reasonably equitable manner—and he suggests his concurrence with efforts to achieve such a common good through his agreement with the position that "the wealth of the community can and may be commandeered for the common good . . . [and] . . . spent by the community for those community values which can be obtained in no other way."[21]

Contrary to Pfuetze, Mead does not suggest that creating a common good from the present social good will be an easily attainable goal, especially as it entails a radical reconstruction or rethinking by individuals of their place within the social framework. "We have become bound up in a vast society," he writes, "all of which is essential to the existence of each one, but we are without the shared experience which this should entail" (SW 301). It is this shared experience, articulated in a conscious fashion, that will enable individuals to move from a feeling of isolation to a recognition of the social nature of contemporary life and eventually to a fostering of the common good. This shared experience, Mead notes, can thus contribute to the feeling that we are all "working toward a common end" (MSS 276) that interpenetrates the particular functions of each individual, then to still further agreements upon the nature of our most pressing social problems, and eventually even the bundle of central needs that comprise human nature.

If at times Mead suggests a goal of "a perfected social intelligence" in which "all social meanings would each be similarly reflected in their respective individual consciousness—such that the meanings of any one individual's acts or gestures . . . would be the same for any other individual whatever who responded to them" (MSS 310), this understanding ought not to be mistaken for a homogenized and mechanized existence. "The world is a different world to each individual," Mead notes, because "the universe from my point of view is different than it is from your point of view" (MT 416). Moreover, these differentiae are too important to be destroyed. One aspect of "a highly developed and organized human society," he maintains, is that it is a society in which "the individual members are interrelated in a multiplicity of different intricate and complicated ways whereby they all share a number of common social interests." But the other side of this society is that the individuals are "more or less in conflict relative to numerous other interests which they possess only individually, or else share with one another only in small and limited groups" (MSS 307). The goal of this modern society is, then, to develop a "full degree" of "functional differentiation and social participation" (MSS 326) such that individuals can share differences with other members of the community, learn from each other, and teach each other new possibilities. Through a focus upon the community, we might be able to foster the adoption of largely overlapping perspectives on human nature and perhaps, as a consequence, the adoption of groups of mutually acceptable goods.

VI

Mead's analysis of collective social action offers us a theory of social change that stresses the possibility of intelligent action to address, to mitigate, and, at times, to solve our collective ills. Although our intelligence always will be qualified and limited by circumstances, some of which we have just examined, this analysis will be better able to help us in our present situation if we see it not as a system or protocol for social reform but simply as an analysis of what an adequate understanding of intelligent social action would be. Mead's analysis might be helpful especially as it precludes excessive expectations and the consequent depressions that necessarily result from the extravagant claims of many other analyses of intelligence. As a society, we are facing severe ills, and we now have neither the inherent flexibility of the pioneer life-style nor the undeveloped space to start over. We need to work together—to go back and try to rebuild our cities and clean our rivers, to retool our factories and salvage our farmlands, to bring adequate education and health care to all. We need to recreate communities. Mead emphasizes that we have the possibility to reconstruct more successfully and effectively if we inquire, adjust, and look to the future consequences for the community with faith in the possibility of success. This sort of social action Mead calls "intelligent."

If we adopt Mead's analysis of intelligent social action, we must admit that such action seems possible. It is not as simple a process as we once thought; it is not as certain a process as we once hoped; and it is not as inexpensive a process as we once pretended. But it can be done. Mead thus denies the claims of critics like Reinhold Niebuhr that because of the high degree of selfishness in humans it is "impossible for them to grant to others what they claim for themselves." Mead also denies Niebuhr's more extreme claim that we can never be fully rational when our own interests are at stake because we use reason "as kings use courtiers and chaplains to add grace to [our] enterprise."²² Mead's work reaffirms the possibility of a higher degree of selflessness than Niebuhr, and others, thought realistic—to the extent that we can make the issues both personal and social. To personalize the issues means taking them from the abstract level and making them "so immediate and practical that they can appear in the minds of the voter as his own problem" (SW 263). Moreover, if we can foster a recognition by the individual of the significance of the growing interrelationship and interdependence of the modern community, this personal focus will not be isolating. This is so, Mead writes, because we can "use this growing consciousness of interdependence to formulate the problems of all, in terms of the problem of everyone" (SW 264).

Mead has outlined the nature of intelligent social action and has suggested the value that such a path of action would have should we follow it. The fact that, as yet, this path has not been adopted does not undermine the validity of his hypothesis. It does, however, call into question the likelihood of its adoption. Thomas Vernor Smith, one of Mead's disciples, was referring to this likelihood when he wrote that it was impossible to uncover in Mead's thought the basis of his optimism regarding social amelioration. Agreeing with Mead that there are possibilities inherent in our modern world—that is, it is "not that we have a perfect world, but that we have the instrument for its perfecting"— Smith still wondered, Why does Mead see "in social intelligence so much greater an instrument for amelioration than other men see?" Smith's answer was that Mead was attempting "to lay an impregnable foundation for ethical and social optimism" and, to this end, simply borrowed from the broader philosophic tradition "enough natural social harmony to swell into a sufficient showing for optimism the little harmony he was able to create."²³

What Smith seems to have overlooked, however, is the importance of the hortatory mood in Mead's social thought. Our possibility of success, in Mead's analysis, is not just related to the efficacy of what Smith described as the instrument for our world's perfecting. It is also related to the possibility of getting individuals to assume moral responsibility for trying to bring about a better world. Mead's focus is thus upon a level of possibility that is influenced by greater or lesser contributions of individuals' time and effort, by our willingness or lack of it to lay duties upon ourselves. It is vitally important to the plausibility of Mead's position that we recognize that we are not passengers on a cruise, but sailors whose efforts influence the outcome of our journey.[24] By making our ethical choices, Mead tells us, "we have more or less definitely determined the character of the situation" (MT 102). When we as citizens decide that certain difficulties are to be addressed while others are not and that certain problems deserve a public response whereas others do not, it is our collective decision that determines the situation. And, most important, when we determine that certain situations are beyond the power of intelligent social action, our resultant decision not to act makes them so.

What Pfuetze has characterized as Mead's acceptance of "a utopian social optimism"[25] would thus be seen by Mead himself as no more than a cautious anticipation of success. Far worse, from Mead's point of view, would be either to have underconfidence in our cooperative possibilities or to hold action in abeyance until we are aided by some suprahuman force. We have been lucky so far; but, as we come increasingly to feel the strain of global limitations, we cannot expect our luck to hold out indefinitely. To the extent that we can act to improve our situation, we have a moral obligation to do so. And this is an obligation that only we can lay upon ourselves. We have to accept the responsibility for our value choices and for the direction of our collective lives. As Mead wrote with regard to the World War I, "We have come far short of accepting that responsibility. We fashioned the marvellous world of the twentieth century, and then undertook within it to fight an eighteenth-century war."[26] In the nearly seventy years since Mead wrote the words cited at the beginning of this chapter, we seem to have again become "pilgrims and strangers." We are not "at home" in the world but rather possessed and controlled by it. What he characterized as "a splendid adventure" if we could but rise to it has become foreboding and terrifying. We have stopped looking for problems because we do not want to see what difficulties will come next; we have stopped adapting because we would rather that others change instead of us; and, most important, we have lost the faith that success is really possible. We have not yet risen to the challenge of Mead and the other Pragmatists to assume responsibility for our own lives. And time grows short.

4

John Dewey's
Method of Social Reconstruction

During his 1932 campaign for the presidency, Franklin Delano Roosevelt called for a more compassionate and vigorous government to wrest the country from the Great Depression. On one occasion he told his fellow citizens: "The country needs and, unless I mistake its temper, the country demands bold, persistent experimentation. It is common sense to take a method and try it: If it fails, admit it frankly and try another. But above all, try something." Later, in accepting the nomination of the Democratic party, he pledged "a new deal for the American people."[1] This promised New Deal was a resolute commitment to replace the stagnation and despair that he found in the Hoover administration with a more dynamic and optimistic approach to government; his campaign, however, remained short on specifics. As one commentator has written, although Roosevelt never clearly indicated what he intended to do in the White House, "at least he promised to do something, and that was enough for millions of voters."[2] Once inaugurated, Roosevelt began a series of more-or-less successful programs through newly created agencies. When a particular course of action failed to work, he abandoned it for another—living up to his pledge to "above all, try something."

The trial-and-error actionism of Roosevelt's political approach is frequently presented as being pragmatic—for example, Arthur M. Schlesinger, Jr., called him "a supreme political pragmatist."[3] Although at times commentators have viewed John Dewey as largely responsible for such political pragmatism,[4] Dewey himself condemned Roosevelt for failing to offer a well worked out and coherent program. The president, Dewey wrote in 1934, was "just messing around": "doing a little of this and a little of that in the hope that things will improve" (LW 11:292–93). Dewey believed that this improvisational approach was inadequate because " 'reforms' that deal now with this abuse and now with that without having a social goal based upon an inclusive plan, differ entirely from effort at re-forming, in its literal sense, the institutional scheme of things" (LW 11:45). In his attacks on the New Deal Dewey indicates, more clearly than at any other time in his career, his belief that an adequate social philosophy must be based in a vision of a satisfactory human life and equipped with a method sufficient to develop a comprehensive program offering specific measures to deal with specific problems.

That Dewey held such a position will no doubt puzzle many readers because we have all heard that, however strong a vision of a satisfactory human good he might have offered, he did not offer specific measures or a comprehensive program and he lacked a method. I would like to demonstrate a number of points about Dewey's Pragmatic social philosophy: that he had a method of translating his vision into a social program and that this method can be uncovered in his work, although he himself never fully elaborated it; that he did suggest many specific measures and the outline of a program; that these particular suggestions, however, are the less important part of his social philosophy, for a number of reasons; and finally, that his method—a two-level method of intellectual and institutional reconstruction—is very important as a means of understanding Dewey's social thought. Along the way, a series of valuable Pragmatic suggestions will emerge for our own day.

II

As I have noted, Dewey has been criticized frequently for not giving answers. Charles Frankel, for example, writes,

> although Dewey argued that philosophy must be a guide to the solution of concrete, practical problems, he repeatedly left his readers guessing what he himself thought about such issues. . . . in his writing he regularly stopped at just the point where we are anxious to see, if only in outline, the kind of practical, positive program he thought his ideas implied. . . . [There should not be] . . . the difficulty there is in determining where Dewey stood, simply as one man among other men, on many of the issues that he himself raised for discussion.[5]

In H. S. Thayer's view, Dewey always draws back at the "crucial point" of prescription, perhaps from "his fear of absolutizing ends" or "his philosophic rejection of static goals" or "his practical mistrust of inflexible social programs." But, Thayer concludes, regardless of Dewey's motivation, "what was wanted but never forthcoming from pragmatists practicing intelligence was a social program, something more concrete and pragmatically meaningful than 'growth' or 'intelligence.' " [6] Finally, we have Morton White's remark that Dewey's approach could unnerve readers "who tired of hearing him constantly talk about the importance of using scientific intelligence in political affairs without hearing him describe concrete political programs."[7] These three commentators are but the most prominent.[8]

A careful examination of Dewey's work, however, gives a very different picture. A brief listing of the sorts of specific practical questions he answered would include the following:

—Should Americans support Woodrow Wilson's war to make the world safe for democracy?
Yes (see MW 10:265–80; MW11:98–106).

—Do Americans have a right, and even a duty, to become involved in Polish politics in Europe and in the United States during this war?
Yes (see MW 11:241–330; MW 398–408).

—How should Western nations prevent further economic and political exploitation of postwar China?
Establish an international commission to control the dealings of Western nations with China (see MW 13:185–90).

—How should Western nations deal with the sudden increase in anti-Oriental prejudice that accompanied the end of the war?
Continue to restrict immigration, at least for a while (see MW 13:242–54).

—Should Americans support the Versailles Treaty and join the League of Nations?
No (see MW 15:78–86, 378–82).

—How should the nations of the world respond to the stupidity and carnage of modern warfare?
Outlaw war.[9]

—Should Americans adopt communism, foster class struggle, and work toward the proletarian revolution as a means of dealing with the Depression?
No (see LW 9:91–95; LW 11:382–86).

—Can Americans then expect that the interplay of the two major political parties will end the Depression and move the country toward progress and justice?

No, a new party is desperately needed (see LW 6:156–89; LW 9:66–70, 76–80).

—If another European war were to break out in 1939, should America get involved in the fighting?
"No Matter What Happens—Stay Out" (LW 14:364).

Dewey also suggested and worked for educational measures too numerous and varied to list here.[10]

These examples of suggested courses of action should be enough to cause Dewey's critics to rethink their position that he always leaves people in the dark. However, if these examples are not enough, we need only recall his associations with three groups of socially active citizens: the League for Industrial Democracy (LID), the League for Independent Political Action (LIPA), and the People's Lobby.[11] Dewey was a longtime spokesman for these organizations, serving at one time or another as president of each. He also wrote for them, suggesting many possible courses of action. In 1934 for the LID, for example, he produced a pamphlet entitled *Education and the Social Order,* which recommended, among other suggestions, that schoolteachers ally themselves with organized labor in order to be able to protect themselves, their students, and their educational programs from budgetary pressures (see LW 9:175–85, 514–15). Immediately after the elections of 1932 we find Dewey, in the *News Bulletin of the L.I.P.A.,* calling for continued efforts by independent voters to strengthen their impact upon the congressional elections of 1934 by "the tenfold multiplication of our local branches" (LW 6:255). He also wrote frequently for the *People's Lobby Bulletin,* which began publication in the depths of the Depression in 1931.

The first years' issues of the bulletin contain a running attack by Dewey on Hoover's economic policies for dealing with the Depression and continued calls for fundamental economic redistribution to address the fact that 4 percent of the American population owned 80 percent of the nation's wealth. He hoped to accomplish this redistribution by means of increased taxes on those with large incomes from investments and by replacing feeble and degrading private charity with immediate increases in federal relief and public works measures like the 1932 Wagner Relief Bill (S.3696) and Wagner Construction Bill (S.4076) (see LW 6:337–400). After the Roosevelt administration took over in early 1933 and began enacting its measures, Dewey's efforts became still more specific. There is, for example, his November 1933 attack upon a series of recently enacted consumption taxes. He continued to call for more jobs, housing, and relief and for a fundamental redistribution of wealth through income taxes upon the wealthy; and, as we saw above, he found Roosevelt's overall approach to be "just messing around." Eventually, Dewey's rejection of Roosevelt's efforts "to save the profit system from itself" culminated in his call for "the socialization of all natural resources and natural monopolies, of ground rent, and of basic industries" because "only elimination of profits through socialization, will prevent eventual chaos" (LW 9:289–90).[12]

It should be clear from this brief survey that, in spite of the opinions of many commentators to the contrary, Dewey did suggest courses of action with regard to matters of both broad and narrow scope. Moreover, were this survey expanded to include the rest of Dewey's many other suggested courses of action, a rather thorough program for social reconstruction would emerge. Of course, we might not accept each of his particular suggestions. Presumably no one but Dewey himself agreed with every one; and, no doubt, were he still living, he would have revised his opinion on at least some of them. He did, in fact, change his mind on several major matters of public concern during his lifetime, three outstanding cases being his decreasing reliance upon war as an acceptable means of international reconstruction, his support of ever-greater levels of social democracy, and his growing recognition of the need for a viable third party. These changed convictions are in accord with his fundamental belief that "every measure of policy put into operation is, *logically,* and *should* be actually, of the nature of an experiment" (LW 12:502), to be modified in practice. Regardless of the hypothetical nature of these positions, however, Dewey did advance them; in failing to adequately understand and report this side of his work, commentators are simply mistaken.

From one point of view, these commentators' failure here would seem to be a very minor mistake, for the specific answers themselves are, in a sense, not extremely important. Under Dewey's method of social reconstruction, the answers to specific questions remain secondary to the method itself, in that proffered courses of action, suggested by himself or others, need to go through a process of cooperative examination and social evaluation before their enactment. The emphasis in this process of examination and evaluation, by means of which the community is to decide upon possible courses of action, is not upon the person who brought forth the plan nor upon the plan's initial plausibility, but upon a thorough measuring of long-term consequences. Thus, since Dewey's specific suggestions for courses of social action are to be seen as nothing more than suggestions,[13] from one point of view, to fail to take account of them would seem to be a minor mistake.

However, from a more important point of view, it is seriously disturbing to see these commentators on Dewey's social thought mistakenly directing their fire at his alleged lack of specific answers. This error is disturbing because these repeated complaints indicate that the commentators believe that his answers are somehow crucial. If these commentators saw more clearly the nature of Dewey's political method, their complaints that he offered us no answers would be abandoned as irrelevant. In their place we would find a critical examination and evaluation of Dewey's method of social reconstruction, because for him the method was primary.

III

As I have suggested, Dewey's approach to social reconstruction emphasizes method, but this emphasis needs to be clarified. We need first to look at Dewey's understanding of method in general. I do not intend here a full-scale exploration of Dewey's sense of method; but, for what is to follow, it is important that we become at least a bit clearer about how he understands method, both in general and in such phrases as "scientific method," "the democratic method," "the method of inquiry," "the method of cooperative intelligence," and so on. Our task, however, is not an easy one. As Justus Buchler correctly notes, "No philosopher of this century has been more closely identified with attention to method than Dewey," although method never received at Dewey's hands "the direct and generalized examination" that it should have.[14] In several of his major volumes Dewey offers such chapters as "The Nature of Method," "The Problem of Method," "Experience and Philosophic Method," "The Supremacy of Method," and "Systematic Method."[15] But these chapters amount more to a series of hints and suggestions than to the thorough analysis of method that is necessary. One possible explanation for his constant emphasis upon method, combined with his failure to analyze it sufficiently, is that his sense of method was so much a part of what he called his "native bent"[16] that he never felt compelled to take valuable time away from addressing problems to analyze it fully. Regardless of the accuracy of this possible explanation, however, we still need to become clearer about what method means for Dewey.

Perhaps it is best to begin our examination of his sense of method by indicating what it does not mean. First, we must recognize that, for Dewey, having a method for social action does not imply having in advance a minutely prepared procedural blueprint or protocol that is to be imposed upon the social realm. It is possible to have a method yet still be flexible and adaptive. As he writes of problem solving in general, a method represents only an outline of "the indispensable traits of reflective thinking" (LW 8:207), not a prearranged schedule of actions. Surely the latter mechanical understanding of method goes beyond mere methodicalness to an unnecessarily rigid and predetermined kind of method.

Similarly, Dewey's sense of method should not be understood to include a system for easily generating solutions to problems based on general principles.[17] Nowhere in any of his discussions of inquiry[18] does he suggest that such a method for generating answers could be developed. On the contrary, Dewey says that "suggestions just spring up, flash upon us, occur to us" (LW 12:113–14). As he explains elsewhere, the direct generating of ideas is impossible because "suggestions just occur or do not occur, depending . . . on the state of culture and knowledge at the time; upon the discernment and experience and native genius of the individual; upon his recent activities; to some extent upon chance" (LW 8:251). We can indirectly influence the occurrence and content of suggested options by controlling situations, but we cannot make them appear in accordance with some direct method. The sense of method that Dewey is offering suggests that we begin to seek direct control only after the appearance of the ideas: "while the original happening of a suggestion, whether it be brilliant or stupid, is not *directly* controlled, the acceptance and use of the suggestion is capable of control" (LW 8:251). Thus humans suggest possible options of uneven quality, as he did, for a whole host of complex reasons; these suggestions can then be tried and tested—adopted, revised, rejected—according to the method that we shall examine below. But there can be no method, Dewey maintains, for generating these ideas. In consequence, he emphasizes the importance of developing indirectly, through education and experience, "the social sensitiveness of the inquirer[s] to the needs and problems of those with whom [they are] associated" (MW 12:165).[19]

So, methodicalness, in the sense that Dewey intends, implies neither the need for a predetermined plan of action nor an easy system for generating quick answers from a general philosophical viewpoint. Turning to consider more closely what he does intend by method, we can point out, with Dewey, that there are many procedures or systems or techniques that, when adopted, will yield answers to problems of social concern. These include following custom or tradition, obeying political authority, accepting some version of divine will, conforming to the wishes of the wealthy and powerful, resorting to partisan politics, and so on.[20] All of these procedures, whatever their value, can and should be considered to constitute methods in some broad sense, for they are ways to organize action toward the goal of a solved problem.[21] Human experience has tried these methods and others, although Dewey considers all of the methods listed here to be inadequate and outdated— vestiges of a time, he writes, "when the practice of knowing was in its infancy" (LW 4:164).

We approach still closer to Dewey's sense of method when we examine various methods to discover "why some methods succeed and other methods fail" (LW 12:17). After granting methodicalness to virtually all procedures for organizing action, he focuses upon evaluating these procedures to determine which are likely to resolve problematic situations and produce desired results. Bad methods are ones that produce "short-cut 'solutions' " that "do not get rid of the conflict and problems; they only get rid of the feeling of it" (MW 12:160). As Dewey writes, "Uncertainty is got rid of by fair means or foul" (LW 4:181). A good method, on the other hand, would "protect the mind against itself" (MW 12:99) by making sure that the doubt was taken advantage of or put to "productive use" (LW 4:182) by inquirers who saw the existence of problems to require changes made through a process of social exploration and evaluation.

As a framework for the exploration of social problems and the evaluation of suggested possible solutions, Dewey modeled his method of social reconstruction upon the method of the natural sciences. The parallels, of course, are not exact: "The question is not whether the subject-matter of human relations is or can ever become a science in the sense in which physics is now a science, but whether it is such as to permit of the development of methods which, as far as they go, satisfy the logical conditions that have to be satisfied in other branches of inquiry" (LW 12:481). And if the relationships between natural science and social science, and between the method of science and broader social method, are nowhere fully worked out in his writings, this may be because, as he suggests, the full development of social science cannot precede "efforts at social control" but must be developed in the process of "putting social planning into effect" (LW 6:66).

Now that we have a better sense of what Dewey intends by a method of social reconstruction, for further understanding we can turn to the question of the explicitness of Dewey's own elaboration of this method of social reconstruction. His limited discussions of method in general should suggest the answer. He does not provide an explicit elaboration of this method in his writings; nowhere does he expressly put forward what I am calling his method of social reconstruction. Nevertheless, he does assume this method and use it in all of his public writings and actions. I have attempted to uncover this method through a thorough exploration of his writings considered in the context of his social situation and of the writings of his fellow Pragmatists, and to elaborate it by rearranging these writings around his central theme of social reconstruction. I believe that this understanding of Dewey makes the most sense of his voluminous and diverse social writings as well as bringing them to their proper place in the forefront of his thought.

IV

The careful study of Dewey's work makes clear that he used a two-level method of social reconstruction, one that we can also use, should we find it adequate, in areas of public concern as diverse as politics, economics, education, religion, and international affairs. This method can be understood as an application of the pattern of inquiry to the social realm that operates roughly as follows: When a social problem arises, doubts and conflicts occur. The community formulates the problem, develops facts, evidence, and explanations, reasons carefully to develop hypotheses, and evaluates these hypotheses through practical social interaction. The first level of this method is largely intellectual; the second is largely practical.[22] At the first level the problem is formulated, and possible solutions are brought forth; at the second level, the community evaluates these possibilities and enacts the chosen solution.

The first level involves a process of problem formulation: gathering information, clarifying the situation, and identifying possible options to help the public "find and identify itself" (LW 2:370). By deliberately focusing upon problems in this way, Dewey hopes to make use of cooperative inquiry on the part of citizens of all intellectual backgrounds and perspectives to effect the necessary solutions. "The actual change in human estate can be brought about," he writes, "only by the cooperative practical efforts of men of good will in all occupations and professions" (LW 16:367). He believes that academic experts, working in conjunction with other perspectives, could be particularly helpful once these experts were no longer "intellectually dispersed and divided" and once they began to focus their efforts on the "issues of stupendous meaning" that confront society (LW 5:107–8). These experts could gather facts and interpret meanings, formulate explanations, and undertake the reasoning that would make our social problems more easily understandable to the public. Finally, they could present hypothetical value choices—both of possible goals that we should seek as solutions to our problems and of the possible means to achieve them (cf. LW 11:14–15). Economists, sociologists, lawyers, biologists—working among others of their own discipline and in conjunction with members of other perspectives—would contribute through their specialties to the process of social reconstruction (cf. MW 12:273–74). The philosopher has a special task to perform in this process of intellectual reconstruction: to examine our ideas, our concepts, and our political perspectives and to see whether they are "intellectually competent to meet the needs of the situation" (MW 15:54). Our particular task, as philosophers, is thus "clarifying certain of the ideas which enter into the discussion" (MW 10:245), thereby helping to determine which of the ideas have failed to keep pace with the process of social change.

The reconstruction of social institutions represents the second level of Dewey's method of social reconstruction. At this level, the interested, active body of citizens evaluates, tests, and enacts the changes suggested to it from the intellectual level. It is not enough to simply develop plans and proposals, suggestions for laws, and outlines of pilot studies. We must evaluate them in social forums, forums that Dewey believed could be established only through the creation or reconstruction of voluntary and official institutions of education and communication. He writes that it is "only by experimental and personal participation in the conduct of common affairs" that we can expect to achieve a "heightened emotional appreciation of common interests" and "an understanding of social responsibilities" (MW 11:57). This participation could be effected in large measure through the creation of "local agencies of communication and cooperation" (LW 13:177) and institutions of "debate, discussion and persuasion" (LW 2:365), both for clarifying and disseminating the opinions of the members of the community. These voluntary agencies could be the means for the tolerant interplay of opinions and the eventual formation of an intelligent consensus. This tolerance is particularly necessary in recognition of our own fallible nature, and particularly justified as a result of Dewey's belief that through cooperative inquiry we can reach eventual agreement (cf. LW 7:329–31).

Some of the agencies for the exchange of ideas and information would include the media, especially newspapers and magazines. Dewey's own work in the latter medium is well known, if insufficiently studied.[23] Other such institutions are the school and its cousin the social settlement or community house. These agencies are places where the possibilities of tolerant and reciprocal interaction of groups are combined with the ongoing possibility of a high level of "deliberate inquiry and discussion" (MW 8:100). In addition, Dewey suggests, if we are to take political choices out of the unwatched hands of political parties we need the development of a new kind of quasi-political organization like the above-mentioned League for Independent Political Action. He describes the LIPA as "a clearing-house" for liberal sentiment and ideas that could serve "to promote education and organization" toward the foundation of a new kind of political party (LW 9:67; cf. LW 5:346–48). Establishment of the kind of party Dewey had in mind would be a fundamental break with our two-party tradition, which he saw as power oriented rather than issue oriented. He described the struggle between our two current parties as "a struggle for immediate power with no one having any idea of what is to be done with the power if it is gained—except to use it again in the next election" (LW 6:162). Dewey believed it would be possible to change this process—to make of our political activity a cooperative inquiry into the problems facing society and the social enactment of programs to deal with those problems.

V

Dewey's method of social reconstruction has important implications for the social question, What role are experts to play in a democracy? Beginning with the condemnation of what has been characterized as "the simple-minded equation between science and democracy,"[24] many commentators maintain that experts have no role to play in a democracy. This is so because, in any political situation, a choice must always be made between *democratic consensus* and what can be broadly characterized as *scientific expertise*. Albert W. Levi, for example, writes that "a scientifically constructed plan can probably not be democratically accepted, and a democratically accepted plan will probably not be scientific."[25] Wilmon H. Sheldon, focusing upon why he believes that democratically accepted plans would not be scientific, maintains that democracy does not lead to intelligent and justifiable choices because "the democratic remedy for human ills does not cure, but inflames, certain sores which rankle in the spiritual anatomy of man."[26] Thus, democracy appeals not to citizens' rationality but to their shortsighted understanding of self-interest. It is because of this aspect of democracy, Walter Lippmann believes, that leaders in democracies "have been compelled to make the big mistakes that public opinion has insisted upon." Thus, far from seeing the democratic method as a means to attain the long-term social good, Lippmann sees it as fatally flawed. "The decisive consideration is not whether the proposition is good but whether it is popular—not whether it will work well and prove itself but whether the active talking constituents like it immediately."[27]

Many commentators thus believe that no workable relationship is possible between consensus and expertise and that it is consequently necessary, for the common good, to take choices out of the hands of the people and place them in the hands of more "rational" experts.

This technocratic position is made explicit by Edward Lee Thorndike: "Wherever there is the expert . . . should we not let him be our guide? Should we not, in fact, let him do our thinking for us in that field?"[28] From such a point of view, experts have no role in democratic decision making; rather their role is to advance social management and control. Thus they take the decisions out of the hands of the people.

Throughout his career Dewey wrote of the values of democracy and of science, and he believed that it was possible to develop a workable relationship between democratic consensus and scientific expertise, one that would have an integral role for the experts. At the heart of this position is his belief that consensus of political opinion and correctness of social policy could very largely overlap. Dewey holds this view because he believes it is possible to introduce the attitudes and findings of specialists and experts into the discussions that take place in the "free gatherings of neighbors on the street corner" and in the "gatherings of friends in the living rooms of houses and apartments" that he thought were "the heart and final guarantee of democracy" (LW 14:227). And, while Frankel was surely correct that "a democratic consensus can be a consensus in illusion,"[29] it need not be. Dewey believes that, through the interaction of specialists and the broader society, a community of active, involved citizens might arise that regularly expected more of itself than just consensus—a community that, with the help of its various experts, would be able to recognize and achieve the common good.

Dewey's understanding of the proper role of experts in a democracy is a complex one. Recognizing that "the world has suffered more from leaders and authorities than from the masses," he is careful to point out that he is not advocating "government by experts" (LW 2:365). But neither is he advocating government without experts. Many of the questions of public concern—for example, "sanitation, public health, healthful and adequate housing, transportation, planning of cities," and so on—are questions with regard to which the experts' opinion plays a large role. To the extent that such problems can be settled by "inquiry into facts" alone—for example, in a case like "the construction of an efficient engine for purposes of traction or locomotion"—the experts' decision should be, with our consent, the decisive factor (LW 2:313). However, deciding the engineering aspects of locomotive construction does not constitute a political question. The political questions involved with locomotives are more likely to be ones such as what the working conditions in the factories and on the rails are to be, where the locomotives should go, their speed and frequency, their type of fuel, whether the transportation system should be self-supporting or taxpayer-subsidized, and so on. These are truly political decisions—decisions that fall outside the realm of expert opinion and thus bring into play "the necessity for the participation of every mature human being in formation of the values that regulate the living of men together" (LW 11:217). These decisions need to be effected at the second level of Dewey's social method, through communal evaluation.

At the second, or institutional, level of social reconstruction, there is no decisive role for experts. In the task of making value choices from among the options that we have before us, there can be no recognition of special expertise because to grant it would be to consign some citizens to an inferior status. For Dewey, "all those who are affected by social institutions must have a share in producing and managing them" (LW 11:218). Public choices must be made in discussions of broad-based groups of citizens of general intelligence who recognize in their experience the needs and possibilities of the society. The average individuals of the society, he writes, may be at present part of a "submerged mass," and they "may not be very wise," he notes facetiously. "But there is one thing they are wiser about than anybody else can be, and that is where the shoe pinches" (LW 11:219). For the process of social reconstruction to be democratic rather than technocratic, the level of institutional reconstruction can allow for no special role for experts.

This two-level analysis, I suggest, is the best way to understand Dewey's formal solution to the problem of the role of experts in a democratic society. Of course, a formal solution does not always yield all necessary practical answers. One practical problem with Dewey's understanding of the role of experts in a democracy has to do with how we determine which issues and sub-issues are to be considered expert-related. The growth of environmental activism on the part of the American populace, for example, must be seen as part of an issue that is being socially redefined as political rather than as a matter of expertise. For many concerned citizens, this redefinition is an indication of social advance. At the same time we must also recognize that the continuing stigmatization of evolutionary thinking by the creationism movement is also an instance—however misguided—of the same process of social redefinition. These two cases indicate that in a democracy presumably any issue must be seen as political, rather than as expert, if a sufficient number of people find its contemporary disposition problematic.

This claim results from the fact that in a democracy the disposition of issues should be decided by the community itself, rather than by experts. On those occasions when we find ourselves decrying the abject stupidity of the mob instead of lauding the sagacity of our citizenry, we must turn our efforts to the improvement of public opinion rather than to strengthening the power of our experts to save us from ourselves.

The attempts of experts to dictate social policy to the rest of the citizens rest in the delusion that social welfare "can consist in a soup-kitchen happiness, in pleasures we can confer upon others from without" (MW 14:202). If Dewey is correct when he writes that political life "is essentially a cooperative undertaking, one which rests upon persuasion" (MW 10:404), then it is part of everyone's task as a concerned citizen, and as an expert in some limited areas, to attempt to influence public opinion. We must thus attempt to inform the other members of the public and to criticize prevailing outlooks that we consider mistaken. By attempting to persuade others to accept what we, although fallible ourselves, believe to be better choices, we formulate issues and decide courses of action in a communal way.

A second practical problem, perhaps more pressing than the first, is that of maintaining the experts in a service role, uninterested in exercising illegitimate power over the rest of society. Dewey's institutionalization of a role for experts—however limited—might be seen (especially by democrats who are skeptical of his claims about the possible integration of democracy and expertise) as the first step toward the replacement of democracy by technocracy. Such a conclusion is certainly one way to read the antidemocratic passages cited earlier. Either because we tend to take experts' advice too seriously, or because the experts themselves do, experts tend to wield an undue amount of influence in our society, and they give ample evidence of a desire to acquire more influence through the further "rationalization" of our social lives.[30] To maintain these experts in a service role will require a great deal of participation on the part of individual citizens, for evaluation and oversight are not possible without familiarity with the problems under consideration, and familiarity is born only of careful study. This does not mean, of course, that each citizen must attempt to master all matters of public concern. But it does mean that each citizen should strive to have an informed understanding of at least one central area—education, the law, ecology, health, the economy, the international picture, and so on—and also some sense of how these areas interrelate.

The criticism that experts might attempt to exert illegitimate social power must be kept distinct from a similar but wrong-headed criticism that *all* attempts to influence and persuade others are essentially manipulative. This sort of criticism is based on an understanding of human nature that is radically different from Dewey's understanding. If individuals know in advance what they need and attempts to change their minds are "infringements" on their rights—and if there is nothing more to act upon than each person's opinion—then, this criticism suggests, all attempts at persuasion must be seen as manipulative and illegitimate.[31] But, if individuals learn their needs and criticize their own desires through interaction, and if attempts to change their minds can be beneficial to them, and if there is some warranting process that can offer us more than just opinion, then, in Dewey's understanding of human nature, attempts at persuasion may be helpful and legitimate.

If we allow for the possibility of legitimate and illegitimate persuasion in society, we still have the practical problem of deciding whether particular instances of persuasion are manipulative or beneficial. Defining manipulation, with C. Wright Mills, as the secretive use of unauthorized power,[32] we would have to admit that experts certainly have the capacity for manipulation and have often exercised it. However, the fault here seems to lie not with Dewey's suggestion that we establish a role for experts, for we could not live as we do today without them. The fault is ours: it lies in our failure to maintain critical control over our experts. Although we recognize with Dewey that no individual or group of individuals "is wise enough or good enough to rule others without their consent" (LW 11:218), we have been all too willing to consent to whatever the experts tell us.[33] We have all too often forgotten that expertise results not from intellectual superiority, and still less from moral preeminence, but from a publicly verifiable method. We have paid dearly for this failure, and until we begin to control our experts we will continue to pay.

VI

Under Dewey's method of social reconstruction, the philosopher, as an expert of a certain sort, has a special role to play through the evaluation of the concepts and ideas that enter into our social discourse. In light of the need to limit the role of experts, it is important to recognize the limited scope of the philosopher's role while emphasizing its importance. In the view of James Gouinlock, "The philosopher can be a most effective *participant* in examining and clarifying moral perplexities and in enlightening our moral struggles, but cannot prescribe solutions to them. He can be most helpful; perhaps a leader, but not a lawgiver."[34] Dewey's understanding of the role of the philosopher in the somewhat broader sphere of social reconstruction is certainly of this sort.

In the social realm, the necessity for the periodic reconstruction of concepts is particularly acute because, Dewey felt, one of the greatest problems in political action is that over time these concepts tend to lose their relevance and become high-sounding phrases. In the words of the coauthor of the *Ethics,* James Hayden Tufts, our conceptions of terms like *justice* and *right* "got their present shaping largely in an industrial and business order when mine and thine could be easily distinguished," but these simpler conceptions are "inadequate for the present order."[35] Dewey explains that conceptions of political terms thus enter into situations "with stubborn and alien characteristics imported from other situations" (MW 4:88), and it is often these "adventitious elements" (LW 11:25) that are seen as the essential, or even the sole, characteristics of the terms. For example, consider the difficulties we as a society have had in coming to grips with the sexual, racial, and economic aspects of democracy when all of our classic formulations arose in a different and simpler world. After a series of great changes during which, as Dewey writes, "an agricultural and rural people has become an urban industrial population" (LW 13:69), it is quite unlikely that earlier understandings of terms like *democracy* or *individualism* would be completely appropriate.

Dewey sees conceptions of political terms as rooted in certain historical contexts because the conceptions themselves are "tools" (MW 15:76) developed and used by political thinkers and actors to deal with particular historical situations. Each conception is thus necessarily partial, for it is rooted in an attempt to resolve a particular problem. Consequently Dewey sees fundamental political terms like *democracy* and *individualism* to be only hypothetically formulatable at any given time. They must undergo reconstruction when a new situation arises.[36] "Like all instrumentalities," he writes, such terms "are modifiable in further use" (LW 12:348). It is thus possible to elaborate what we might call the career of a political conception from the time when it was an idea in the mind of an individual, to whom it seemed to be the answer to a particular political problem, through a period of more-or-less widespread acceptance, to the time when it is abandoned by the society as no longer adequate. To the extent that the conception works as a tool for the solution of a problem, this specificity and interrelation with the situation is necessary and ideal; to the extent that they tie the conception to a particular and dissimilar situation, they lead in the long run to its inability to be useful in answering new problems.

One reason why our conceptions of political ideas so often become merely habitual—that is, passively accepted from current societal usage—is that instead of being seen as tools to solve specific problems they are viewed, and presented, as eternal verities: "immutable truths good at all times and places" (LW 11:26). To the extent that political thinkers see themselves to be dealing with "essential Truth and Reality viewed under the form of eternity," they will be addressing "contemporary problems of living" with at least partly outdated habitual conceptions. "The witness of history is that to think in general and abstract terms is dangerous; it elevates ideas beyond the situations in which they were born and charges them with we know not what menace for the future" (MW 8:143–44). When these conceptions are regarded as "*truths* already established and therefore unquestionable," when they are "not framed with reference to the needs and tensions existing at a particular *time* and *place,* or as methods of resolving ills *then* and *there* existing," they are useless to us in our attempts at solving problems (LW 12:499). Once abstracted, these conceptions, which in their own day and place might have been regarded as liberal or progressive, can become obstructions to what must be done.

In our political conceptions, as well as our moral ideals, Dewey writes, we live in the past. These traditional conceptions of democracy and so forth "are more than irrelevant. They are an encumbrance" (LW 5:86) to the sort of changes that must occur to make our political progress possible. Thus it is that, for example, "the slogans of the liberalism of one period often become the bulwarks of reaction in a subsequent era" (MW 15:76). The task of the philosopher is thus to forestall the petrification of our conceptions of political ideas and to advance the cooperative process of developing conceptions of our political ideas that will be useful to us in our attempts at social reconstruction.

Useful conceptions of political terms must be considered hypothetical. They must "have a directive function in control of observation and ultimate practical transformation of antecedent phenomena," and they must be "tested and continually revised on the ground of the consequences they produce in existential application" (LW 12:499). Thus with regard to any particular political term, in no way is "its most specific historical usage" to be considered "the only legitimate one" (LW 14:252). As George Herbert Mead notes, each of our formulations must be seen as "a *working* conception" (SW 154) of the fundamental idea, as a tool for the adequate understanding of *democracy* or *individualism,* and not as a final, complete formulation of what these terms mean. We must therefore commit ourselves, Dewey writes, to a "continuous reconstruction" of these conceptions "in their intimate connection with changes in social relations" (LW 11:292). Only in this way can we put "a new practical meaning in old ideas" (LW 14:226).

We must abandon the quest for final answers in terms of what our fundamental political ideas *used to mean* in practice because the human situation then and the possibilities then were different. We must abandon the quest for final answers in what our fundamental political ideas *mean in the abstract* because these meanings must be made specific to be usable. Consequently we should search for what our fundamental political ideas like democracy and individualism *mean now in our situa-*

tions (and, to the extent that politics is related to morals, what they could and should mean here and now). As Dewey recognizes, this philosophers' task is perhaps a small factor in making the world a better place, but it is "an indispensable condition of straightening out [the] objective political and economic forces" (MW 15:54).

Consider the political term *individualism*. All who are familiar with Dewey's work will recall the importance he places upon the individual, especially the individual as the agent of social reconstruction. We saw above his emphasis upon "the social sensitiveness" of inquirers. He writes, in a similar fashion, that "individuals are the finally decisive factors of the nature and movement of associated life" (LW 14:91). In our ongoing attempts to advance the common good, he tells us, we must learn to direct the many changes that are occurring in society; this direction and the resultant "quality of change, is a matter of individuality" (LW 14:113). But such individuality is hard to cultivate, Dewey believes, in the social context of an outdated conception of individualism that maintains the following: that individuals are finished prior to social interaction, that freedom from interference is the highest personal good, and that individuals' attempts to advance personal self-interest will lead to both individual and social betterment. Consequently a large portion of Dewey's efforts at conceptual reconstruction—in *Individualism, Old and New* and elsewhere—was directed at developing a new understanding of individualism: one emphasizing personal growth through social interaction, the value of community efforts, and educational attempts to help people become better evaluators and more deliberate seekers of the common good.

People, Dewey writes, will be able to find themselves "only as their ideas and ideals are brought into harmony with the realities of the age in which they act" (LW 5:75). This task requires thorough reconstructions of various political terms like *democracy* and *individualism*—reconstructions carried on in a tentative and hypothetical fashion, rooted both in our traditions and in our current situations—to transform these terms into tools adequate to our needs. The evaluation and reconstruction of political terms is a large and important task, a task in which philosophers have a primary, although not sole, responsibility. This conceptual reconstruction is also an important part of the larger social task of intellectual reconstruction to help society formulate the problems it faces and to clarify its options for public discussion, evaluation, and choice. It is, Dewey writes, "a vital matter" that philosophers have "an active share in developing points of view and outlooks which will further recognition of what is humanly at stake and of how the necessary work may be initiated" (LW 16:380).

VII

Having clarified the implications of Dewey's method of social reconstruction above, it is now possible to begin to criticially examine the contemporary worth of his method. We must wonder why, in particular, if Dewey was correct when he wrote over one half-century ago that "intelligence after millions of years of errancy has found itself as a method" (LW 11:65), our current social situation seems to be little better than the one he faced. If this method of social reconstruction is of value, why has it not been more successful in favorably ordering social change?

One possible explanation for the fact that Dewey's method of social reconstruction has not been as successful as he anticipated it would be is that he himself never displayed it carefully enough to make it widely accessible. That is, perhaps the method was simply unclear to potential users and hence went unused. As we saw above, the problems that many commentators have had in understanding Dewey's method suggest that this explanation is not without some merit. Another possible explanation is suggested by Dewey's own recognition that habits are able to "perpetuate themselves" (MW 14:88). "The force of habit that leads individuals to cling to that which has been established is a genuine part of the constitution of individuals. In the main, it is a stronger and deeper part of human nature than is desire for change" (LW 11:133–34). Thus, given the habits of deference to authority established in people's minds and in the minds of those in authority, as part of any inherited social situation—for example, habits that favor tradition or nation or religion or wealth or political party or whatever—any new method of addressing social problems faces an uphill struggle toward adoption. This neglect of Dewey's method is, however, correctable; and, to the extent that nonuse is the key to his method's lack of success, we could expect that it would become more successful in the future.

I would suggest, however, that no explanation based on our simple failure to understand and use Dewey's method can be fully adequate. To discover why Dewey's method of social reconstruction has not been more successful, and to determine what aspects of it should be and might be revived, it is necessary to explore the fundamental assumptions that underlie Dewey's understanding of our social existence. By examining these assumptions carefully, it will be possible to determine how *appropriate* the method itself is to our actions in the social realm. The import of these assumptions is that we live our lives in (or on the verge of) clusters of democratic communities: larger and smaller, overlapping and telescoping, groups of concerned and active individuals who seek the *common good* in a *democratic way*. In our simple everyday interactions and also in our social conflicts over severe social problems, in which powerful groups lock horns over some vital issue, we must have a sense of the common good as our goal and the democratic process as our means. Dewey's method of social reconstruction thus can be appropriate only to the extent that we address political action as a kind of cooperative experimentation—and not, as C. Wright Mills described the typical social conflict, as "two social interests in a death-clutch."[37]

Dewey is no fool, of course; he had a clearer sense of America's social problems than most other individuals of his day—academic or not. And he is most emphatic in his recognition of social conflict. "Of course, there *are* conflicting interests," he writes. "Otherwise there would be no social problems" (LW 11:56). But he insists that there is an ultimate common good to be sought as the resolution to social problems: "every serious political dispute turns upon the question whether a given political act is socially beneficial or harmful" (LW 2:245). In Dewey's view, social conflicts are irremediable through cooperation only in the case of social problems based in a severe imbalance of power that gives rise to wanton human exploitation—cases where "the interests of all" cannot be simultaneously advanced because they are in conflict, and thus the interests of the few are to be sacrificed in the interests "of the great majority" (LW 11:56). Only in cases of social conflict like these does Dewey find the use of force to be justifiable (see LW 11:61).

Dewey believes in the possibility of a common good; that is, that one day we as a society could become one people, and that even now we can legitimately speak of collective social progress, achievable through the ongoing rational process of "adjusting groups and individuals to one another" (LW 2:355). This process will be fully successful, however, only within a community—a vital one where democracy is not just a type of government but "a way of personal life . . . a moral ideal" (LW 14:228). For Dewey, we remain ever on the threshold of this fuller democracy, barred from closer approach only by our own lack of effort. This effort requires a kind of faith in the possibility of success, faith in the worthwhileness of activities beyond the guarantees of past social experience. For Dewey, this faith in democracy is the root of his melioristic belief that whatever social conditions exist at any given time, "be they comparatively bad or comparatively good, in any event may be bettered" (MW 12:181–82). It is similarly the root of his belief that approaching our problems through cooperative experimentation will advance the common good in the most efficient manner possible.

If we are to evaluate Dewey's method of social reconstruction accurately, it is to these democratic assumptions—not to unclarity or nonuse—that we must turn. We must focus upon his consideration of political action as a kind of cooperative experiment for communally developing a program to advance the common good. Dewey's method of social reconstruction makes sense only when it is rooted in these assumptions. Otherwise, experimentation is time wasted; and cooperation, self-sacrifice. These democratic assumptions operate, moreover, throughout his philosophy, not just in his political thought. His understanding of human nature, his attempts to reconstruct moral theorizing and action, his work to reconstruct educational ideas and institutions, and so on, are all based upon these same democratic assumptions—assumptions that he shared with the other Pragmatic social thinkers. In the chapters that follow, I will begin the long process of trying out these Pragmatic assumptions in our contemporary situation, a process that I hope will demonstrate as well a great deal of the value in Pragmatic social thought.

5

Politics and
Conceptual Reconstruction

Political rhetoric moves in phases. At present, one strong phase is the rhetoric of restoration. Over the last few years we have been hearing a lot about returning our overextended and misdirected government to its "legitimate" tasks, about the importance of recalling that equality "really" refers only to equivalent opportunities and not to the relative evenness of results, about the unnecessary strictures that have been placed upon "valid" property rights, and so forth. In general, we have been hearing a great deal about getting our democracy back in "proper" working order. A primary implication of much of this oratory is that we have been led astray in our social actions by mistaken understandings of key political ideas: of what a government "actually" is, of what equality "really" means, of what owning property "legitimately" entails, of the "true" interpretation of democracy. The suggestion we are being offered is that, once we have reintroduced the "correct" historical understandings of government, equality, property, democracy, and so on, and returned our institutional practices to conform to these "correct" conceptions, we will be back on the "proper" track as a society. This suggestion is mistaken.

The rhetoric of restoration is firmly grounded in an outdated cosmology that places the human drama on a finished stage and gives it a prepared script, a script emphasizing that human nature is fundamentally selfish. Under this view human beings are corrupt and grasping, and their desires need to be bounded by the restraints of traditional morality. Their pride and their pretensions need to be undermined by a recognition of their low ranking within the order of existence, and their aversion to voluntary restraints must be superseded by compulsory

duties and responsibilities. Under this view, too, human beings are de-
luded by the futile goal of human perfectibility, and their endless attempts at innovation must be supplanted by a recognition of the importance of tradition and continuity.

Readers may supply still more aspects of this understanding of human
nature.[1] I think that it is apparent by this point, however, how it un-
dergirds the rhetoric of restoration: under this view human beings attempt to pervert the meanings of key political terms for their own
benefit, and this selfish distortion must be resisted by a defense of the
terms' "correct" meanings.[2] My purpose in this chapter is to offer an
alternative to these understandings of human nature and of political
language. The Pragmatic understanding that I wish to explore arises
from an evolutionary cosmology—a cosmology that emphasizes process,
adaptation, and reconstruction throughout human experience, including political language. Under this evolutionary view human beings are
complex social problem solvers who modify their lives to fit new situations, and their conceptions of the meanings of political terms are
situational: they are hypothetically constructed to fit certain circumstances, and they are instruments for advancing political action. When
faced with a political problem, the evolutionary attitude would reject
the goal of restoring "correct" conceptions of terms or "proper" roles
for government. Rather, this attitude would turn to social reconstruction to solve the problem, attempting to discover new aspects of our
political ideas and new applications of our social institutions. In the
process of social reconstruction it is important to know the past, of
course, but it is just as important to remember that the past *is* past and
that we must continue to adapt ourselves to developing circumstances.

It is indeed true that we can follow the rhetoric of restoration and
reintroduce older conceptions of government, equality, property, and
democracy, as well as older conceptions of individualism, freedom, and
so forth. (It is even true, unfortunately, that this work has been accomplished in large measure already.) But it remains an open question
whether, as the proponents of this orthodoxy maintain, we are in this
way actually restoring "correct" understandings of these terms and
thereby assuring future social success. I would suggest that, on the
contrary, conceptions of our key political ideas are of situational, and
hence varying, import. Because our social and political conditions are
now so different from what they once were, the reintroduction of these
older conceptions will neither reestablish past good times—which, as we
know, are vastly overestimated anyway—nor add to the likelihood of
future good fortune. What this self-styled restoration will accomplish,

however, is a reversion of political discourse to a less adequate level and thereby a retrogression in political responsiveness.

II

We can see the reconstructive approach to political language emerging in the thought of a number of American evolutionary thinkers. For example, Oliver Wendell Holmes, Jr., wrote in 1918, "A word is not a crystal, transparent and unchanged, it is the skin of a living thought and may vary greatly in color and content according to the circumstances and the time in which it is used."[3] There is no search here for unchanging correct meanings of words because, Holmes believed, there are none. Circumstances and times are a part of every conception of political terms, and we must not abandon this contextualism in search of some transcendent correct definition. A few years earlier, Walter Lippmann had written in a similar fashion that "words, theories, symbols, slogans, abstractions of all kinds are nothing but the porous vessels into which life flows, is contained for a time, and then passes through."[4] Here we see again the importance of social contexts and directions to understanding and using political terms. To get a fuller sense of the evolutionary mentality and of the reconstructive approach to political language it is necessary to examine more closely four major evolutionary thinkers: William James, Charles Horton Cooley, John Dewey, and George Herbert Mead.

James wrote frequently of the problem of attempting to understand complex human phenomena through definitions, which can reflect at best only partial experience. If we are seeking to define *government,* for example, and we were to ask several different individuals to do so, James writes, "One man might tell us it was authority, another submission, another police, another an army, another an assembly, another a system of laws; yet all the while it would be true that no concrete government can exist without all these things, one of which is more important at one moment and others at another." Consequently, to James's way of thinking, "The man who knows governments most completely is he who troubles himself least about a definition which shall give their essence" and strives for "an intimate acquaintance with all their particularities in turn." Thus, it is "foolish to set up an abstract definition . . . and then proceed to defend that definition against all comers"; and, perhaps more significant, James writes that to view abstract terms "as positively excluding all that their definition fails to include" is to fall into "the vice of intellectualism."[5]

In James, then, we have a recognition of the primacy of the fullness of flowing experience over abstract definitions and a rejection of the need to trim our lives to fit the pattern of limited discourse. However, even in his analysis the problem of understanding political terms seems to be portrayed in a somewhat static fashion, suggesting that if we were to ask enough people or to give a thorough enough definition we would understand all of what democracy or government might mean. His emphasis, at least in the case of political language, is more upon recognizing a plurality of possibilities than upon development within these possibilities. His analysis thus seems to retard the recognition that democracy or government could evolve new aspects.

On this point, a more adequate analysis is offered by Charles Horton Cooley in his discussions of defining what he calls "ideals" like progress, truth, or democracy. All definitions, he writes, ought to be seen as being "in their nature, short-lived," and any endeavor "to produce unmistakable and final definitions" of such ideals ought to be abandoned. He continues that "we have come to recognize that the good, in all its forms, is evolved rather than achieved, is a process rather than a state." The "best definition" of such an ideal, then, is "perhaps nothing other than the most helpful way of thinking about it." For example, "the most helpful way" to understand freedom at any given time, he writes, is "to regard it in the light of the contrast" between what a person "is" and what that person "might be."[6] Cooley, like James, recognizes the error of placing primacy in the definition, but he goes still further and emphasizes the processive, and hence ultimately incomplete, nature of our attempts at defining ideals. But much of his position remains sketchy, as does James's. The suggestions we have encountered thus far are more completely developed in the work of two other Pragmatic thinkers: John Dewey and George Herbert Mead, who offer us a general theory of conceptual reconstruction as a means of filling in the contemporary meaning of abstract political ideals.

This process of conceptual reconstruction is placed by Pragmatic social thinkers within the context of a larger, many-phased process of social reconstruction. They believe that to solve a social problem it is necessary for us not only to act differently but to think differently. From the discovery of an imbalance within the social situation, through its formalization as an addressable problem, to the testing of hypothetical solutions by democratic means, analysis is necessary to determine the contemporary adequacy of our political concepts. Their analysis of conceptions of the meanings of key political ideas as hypothetical, pluralistic, and processive is very different from, and far superior to, what we find in the rhetoric of restoration.

III

Both Dewey and Mead believe that the tendency of the meanings of key political terms to become narrowed and outdated over time is one of the greatest problems for the political theoretician. Unless we are careful, the multiple possibilities within a particular political idea like democracy, for example, can be narrowed to some single habitual conception of it—for example, a conception that contains no requirement of economic democracy—and much of the value of a full understanding of democracy can be lost. In a similar fashion, our understanding of a political idea like democracy can be too closely tied to a particular historical stage—perhaps our party system as a means of effecting political involvement—a habitual stance that hampers the development of a fuller democracy under new circumstances. As a result, our political ideas enter into new and different situations restrained and encumbered by accidental elements derived from earlier situations. The extent to which our political language is inappropriate to our situations is perhaps a minor problem in the short run; but, over longer stretches of time, and through complex and sweeping changes, it can become critical.

Rejecting the immutable cosmology that underlies the understanding of the meanings of these terms as changeless and fully specifiable, Dewey and Mead emphasize that our key political ideas must be seen as being open to multiple interpretations reflecting changes in our circumstances and our self-understanding. Particular conceptions of these political terms, they believe, are established only negatively, as the result of encountering some particular political problem. "Life, liberty, security, property, and even the pursuit of happiness took on a definite connotation from the dangers and hindrances men sought to eliminate," Mead writes (SW 151). Aspects of these conceptions are then situational, and in new situations some modifications are necessary. As a result, we will find ourselves developing over time new definitions of each of these terms.

So, rather than seeing these conceptions of political ideas as unchanging verities, it is better to view them as "tools" (MW 15:76) for refining the material of experience and for solving particular problems. Rather than seeing ourselves as attempting to recognize the antecedently "correct" meanings of political terms, we need to see ourselves as attempting to discover what particular terms might best mean within our particular situations. For example, what might a full conception of democracy be in our situation? Here, as elsewhere in existence, there is novelty. New understandings emerge when new experiences are encountered. New situations indicate the weaknesses and inadequacies of our past formulations (see PP 14–15).The meanings of our key political ideas change because, like other tools, they develop with ongoing use. In the process of problem solution—in the interplay between citizens, each suggesting the recognition of certain ills and advocating certain responses to them—we hammer out a cluster of interdependent conceptions of terms like *democracy, liberty,* and *community* with which we can live for the present. Each of these interdependent conceptions is a stage in the evolution of our understandings of these key political ideas, and collectively they form a dialectical and processive whole (cf. MW 12:187–88; LW 12:348).

Thus each particular conception of a political idea has a kind of lifespan. Each arises in the experience of an individual or group of individuals who see it as the tool to solve a particular felt difficulty. The conception gains support through a process of acceptance and modification, and, if found particularly useful, it can become the dominant conception of that political idea within the community. At each stage it is the specificity of the conception of the political term to the life of the community that leads to its success. Eventually, however, every conception is rendered inadequate by social change and must be reconstructed.

For example, one key political term that Dewey and Mead saw in dire need of reconstruction was *individualism.* Preeminent in their day was an inherited understanding of the individual as somehow independent of social existence—not developing through a process of social give-and-take but predetermined in accordance with some inner plan. Thus individuals must be strongly safeguarded from the interference of other members of society, and especially from the government. Freed to live their own independent lives and pursue their own interests, individuals are able to advance their own and the collective welfare.

The patent inadequacy of this conception as a complete formulation of what individualism means was obvious to Dewey and Mead. This understanding, whatever its past value, amounted in the modern, interrelated world to an individualism for the powerful, an individualism by means of which some individuals were able to live as they saw fit without regard for others. For Dewey and Mead, the individual is essentially social in nature. And, because they see full individualism as an ongoing process of development, they focus upon the means necessary for the creation and maintenance of social individuals. As Dewey writes, "the full freedom of the human spirit and of individuality can be achieved only as there is effective opportunity to share in the cultural resources of civilization" (LW 11:295). A full individualism in their day required institutions to provide education, health care, sanitary advances, employment, and so on to all, and this position directly challenged the inherited understanding of individualism.

Essential to our willingness to reconstruct terms like *individualism* is a willingness to challenge our cultural inheritance to prove its contemporary worth. This spirit runs counter to at least two tendencies of human nature. One tendency is our failure to appreciate our habitual nature, which, Dewey and Mead remind us, in large measure constitutes the self. The other tendency is our failure—perhaps better described as our reluctance—to see these conceptions as tools we have created to solve particular problems. Because of our powerful need to feel justification for our actions, we prefer to see our conceptions of political ideas as having come from on high rather than from the give-and-take of political action, situated in a particular context and simplified in the process of debate. A parallel case of this need can be seen in our desire to think that national boundaries reflect permanent and natural borders rather than the accidents of the historical process. In both of these cases, our desire to seek suprahuman justifications can lead to problems. In the domain of political language, denying the specific origins of our conceptions of political ideas raises them out of the realm of human artifice and denies to them adaptability. Once they are abstracted and sanctified in this way, they will become obstructions to our attempts at adaptation to the new situations we face.

If conceptions of political ideas are to be useful in our broad task of social reconstruction, we must be willing to use them experimentally to modify situations and to see them as open to continuous modification. Thus the most specific historical usage of any political term we have inherited cannot be considered simply as the only legitimate one. Historical usages and current conceptions must be compared and evaluated before we can decide on a present meaning. We cannot be satisfied with simply repeating what democracy or individualism was formerly thought to mean. These conceptions functioned in a largely different world. In the words of James Hayden Tufts, "The older conceptions of liberty and equality need to be enlarged by the constructive attitude of the inventor, by the flexibility fostered by economic processes, and by the differences in interests and values which occupational and economic groupings bring about."[7] To be adequate to our task of social reconstruction, it is necessary for us to continue to search for current weaknesses in our conceptions of our key political ideas—inherited restrictions that our understanding of liberty does not challenge and significant social choices that our understanding of democracy does not include—and to address these ills to prevent present and future suffering. By studying our own situation, and the situations of other cul-

tures, we can come to recognize fuller and more appropriate conceptions of these ideas. And, having recognized what democracy or
individualism might mean in our community, we can and should attempt
to actualize these new meanings.

IV

What are the implications of this Pragmatic position on conceptual
reconstruction for our present political circumstances? If it is true that
neither democracy, nor freedom, nor individualism, nor any other political idea has a fully specifiable meaning, how should this affect our
political discourse? One possible response would be a deliberate choice
on our part to avoid such terms in political discussions because of their
imprecision and consequent likelihood of misinterpretation. This unwise
stricture, although it has certain valuable parallels in nonpolitical discourse, needs to be examined a bit more closely. First, however, we
need to consider a more fundamental question: If these political terms
are without fully specifiable meanings, how are we to maintain workable
boundaries for their legitimate employment?

Should this Pragmatic position suggest that, once we have turned
from tradition as our indicator of the content of political terms, we
cannot evaluate the adequacy of any new formulations? Have we, for
example, entered that fairyland where the prefacing of the name of any
institution with *people's* or *national* or *community* is to be accepted at
face value as demonstrating broad-based democratic participation, or
where the simple use of the term *free*, as in *free market* or *free enterprise*,
should suggest the fullness of liberty? Surely not. New conceptions of
political ideas can and must be evaluated. The point of the Pragmatic
analysis is simply that we cannot continue to evaluate these conceptions
as we have so often in the past: by appeals to abstract definitions or to
our traditional understandings. Of course, it is always possible to define
these political terms abstractly—*democracy*, for example, as 'government
by the people.' Similarly, it is a feasible task, though somewhat more
difficult, to determine what democracy has traditionally meant.[8] However, it is clear that efforts such as these do not complete our evaluative
task.

Our own collective history suggests some of the entanglements that
lurk in the phrase *government by the people*. Which persons are to count
as people, and which are not? How are they to be counted under our
complex federal system? And then there is the problem of accountability
within the representative system. Other problems include the possible

need for constitutional protections against majority tyranny, procedures for undoing past actions, and so on.

There is also the recognition, which has become clearer in recent years, that the narrowly political understanding of democracy that we have inherited is no longer acceptable. As Dewey writes, when democracy is understood as "a way of life" rather than an abstract legal term, what it requires is "the participation of every mature human being in formation of the values that regulate the living of men together" (LW 11:217). Full democracy is now recognized to include participation in decisions in many realms—industrial, medical, scientific—that it was not seen to include even a few years ago. Who is to decide, for example, when factories should be closed down and workers abandoned? How are precious medical facilities and procedures to be allocated? Who should decide on the expansion, or even the continuance, of nuclear power stations or on the means of waste disposal? "The very idea of democracy, the meaning of democracy, must be continually explored afresh," Dewey writes (LW 11:182). It "has to be worked out in terms of needs, problems and conditions of the social life of which . . . we are a part, a social life that is changing with extreme rapidity from year to year" (LW 13:299). We cannot continue to be satisfied with traditional understandings of these terms or with nonspecific abstract definitions.

What this bodes for the future of democracy is clear: an ongoing process of reinterpretation and revision, of specific expansions and specific contractions in its scope, an ongoing process of conceptual reconstruction. What this bodes for the future of political discourse is also clear. We need to turn our focus away from the abstractions of definition and the limitations of tradition to an emphasis upon the unexplored possibilities inherent in our political ideas. In exploring these different possibilities, definitions, and traditions—our own and those of others—can offer us no more than suggestions. It is both interesting and important to know what has been thought and done—but to know this alone is not enough. We need a clear understanding of our present situation and the possibilities it contains for the human good. This understanding can arise only from an adequate vision of human need and potential. It cannot come from the past alone.

We also need to recognize that we have not abandoned democracy or equality, or any of our other vital political ideas, when we set about reconstructing our contemporary conceptions of them. We are not simply making up new meanings for these terms, as some might suggest. Rather, we are reattaching our political ideas to the specific situations under which we live, formulating what these fundamental ideas imply here and now. We must do so without haste or arrogance. We must recognize our place within the community of human inquirers and attempt to comprehend what Mead called "the voices of the past and of the future" (MSS 168). But we must keep our political conceptions in touch with our political reality. We cannot deny the need for ongoing conceptual reconstruction.

Now, to return to the other theme: if it is true that we must continually reconstruct our conceptions of key political ideas, would it not simply be more intelligent to abandon the old terms and adopt new ones? Would we not be wiser in the long run to surrender the old terms to their dated conceptions rather than trying to reinterpret them for present circumstances? For example, might not Dewey have been better off abandoning the term *individualism* rather than replacing the old meaning with a new one, however appropriate and valuable the new meaning seemed to be? Some thinkers, perhaps less concerned with the inherently processive nature of political and other concepts, emphasize the tactical problems with conceptual reconstruction. Their suggestion is conceptual replacement: starting over with new terms.

Conceptual reconstruction, as these critics see it, adds unnecessarily to the confusion of discourse. Morton White, for example, criticizes "the folly of trying to change the usage of words which have well-fixed political meanings."[9] Similarly, Thomas Vernor Smith wrote, "It represents verbal economy and mental clarity to surrender terms when their normal meaning and natural content is gone."[10] Discounting the implied significance of the terms' *normal meaning* and *natural content,* as a general rule this is no doubt excellent tactical advice. Even if we accept Santayana's claim "Philosophy seems to be richer in theories than in words to express them in," we need to be more cognizant, as he was, that "much confusion results from the necessity of using old terms in new meanings."[11] Most philosophical ideas allow for conceptual replacement, and, even in the face of the known risks of using new terms—for example, misinterpretation and isolation from others—we should take Peirce's advice "to coin new terms"[12] and avoid the unnecessary reuse of older terms in philosophical discourse. In this regard, we would do well to remember Dewey's own misfortunes with the conceptual reconstruction of such key philosophical terms as *metaphysics, experience,* and *god*—terms that he later felt compelled to abandon precisely because others repeatedly confused his new conceptions of them with older ones.[13]

In the political realm, however, as distinct from the philosophical, terms function a bit differently, reflecting the differing natures of the inquiries themselves. For this reason, we should be more cautious about adopting new terms in the political realm. We are not as concerned here with precision of formulation or with the universal acceptance of particular meanings and definitions as we are in philosophical discourse. Nor are we as vitally concerned in political discourse with the historical accuracy of our uses of our collective past as we must be when we make claims about our philosophical traditions. Our aim in political discourse, to sketch very broadly, is to develop a working body of sufficient communal spirit that social cooperation is possible and then to help direct that community toward perceived social goods. Much of this task of development and direction is a rhetorical task, and most of our tools in this endeavor are symbolic. Primary among these rhetorical symbols are political terms like *democracy, freedom,* and *individualism.* It is of supreme importance, then, that we do not simply abandon these political terms to their older conceptions and, therefore, to the defenders of these older conceptions. Rather, we must offer new conceptions of what *democracy, freedom,* and *individualism* can and should mean here and now so that these terms can continue to function as useful symbols in our attempts at social reconstruction.

V

How, then, are we to understand our present political situation—a situation in which we are enjoined to return to the "correct" understandings of our key political ideas as a precondition for the reestablishment of "proper" political activity? The analysis of Pragmatic social thought that we have just examined suggests that the present power of the rhetoric of restoration betrays a popular misunderstanding of the nature of definition. Because of this misunderstanding, certain formulations of ideas such as democracy, equality, property, and government have been pulled out of our collective experience and given a primacy that is unjustifiable in light of the historical record and unwise in terms of likely future consequences. Why these particular conceptions have been chosen rather than others of equal historical and intellectual merit has to do primarily with attempts by some individuals to enhance the role of certain felt values that these particular conceptions incorporate. For example, the perceived value of a small government is validated by a conception of democracy that is narrowly political, a conception of freedom as "freedom from interference," and a conception of individualism that maintains, as Dewey puts it, that the person is "something ready-made" (LW 11:30). Perhaps most significant, then, what we have in the present rhetoric of restoration is the use of certain narrow conceptions of key political ideas as tools (perhaps weapons would be a better characterization) in an attempt to reorder our social priorities in accordance with a particular vision of the human good.

Regardless of any merit this vision of the human good might contain—for example, a renewed emphasis upon the importance of individual responsibility—the contemporary attempt to advance it through this method is a misguided one. By their analysis of conceptions of political ideas as categorical, the proponents of this literalism fail to understand the nature of conceptions of political ideas as hypothetical, as attempted solutions to felt problems. By their denial of the functional nature of their own definitions, they fail to account for the operation of conceptions of ideas like democracy and justice as what Dewey calls "political war-cries" (LW 2:326),[14] although this rhetorical use is one of the major ways in which they themselves employ these terms. Similarly, by their assertion of the monistic nature of the "correct" conceptions of these political ideas, they attempt by linguistic sleight-of-hand to deny the pluralistic possibilities inherent in our political ideas. And by their emphasis upon past understandings of political ideas, they undercut the possibility of historical growth in our understandings of these ideas.

It is here that we can see the importance of the Pragmatic analysis of the relationship of conceptual reconstruction to political activity. This analysis recognizes that political ideas have an essentially rhetorical aspect. Similarly, our conceptions of these political ideas are also tools for solving specific felt problems. Because of the functional nature of political conceptions, multiple conceptions are the rule. Democracy, for example, has various characterizations, none of which is to be taken as complete. Finally, with our conceptions of political ideas we are free to expand upon past understandings of the ideas, to recognize the possibilities suggested in new situations. It is by making use of this understanding of the role of conceptual reconstruction in politics that we can maintain and expand political responsiveness—and it is only by means of political responsiveness that the citizens of any democracy can hope to construct a good life for themselves.

6

Freedom and Community

Democracy lives in an intricate balance of liberty and equality. As democratic society moves on, it emphasizes at one time the various aspects of freedom, at another the various aspects of community. For a twenty-five-year period beginning about mid-century, America was the scene of a series of clashes over deeply rooted inequalities in our democratic society and how to address them so that life could be more fulfilling. Particularly with regard to matters of race and gender, we questioned and we modified the way we choose our leaders and our police officers, the make-up of our school curricula and the make-up of our neighborhoods, and the role of government in various social processes. These changes, all enacted in the interest of greater democracy, compromised the available freedoms of many and threatened the potential freedoms of others. But now the flow of our society has moved on, and this emphasis upon equality—whether because of the excesses or half-heartedness of its proponents or because of the astuteness or selfishness of its opponents—is behind us. In the interest of greater democracy, we are at present engaged in an attack on egalitarianism grounded in freedom. Democratic America has once again become the land of liberty where people value most highly the ability to do what they want, unhampered by interference or restraint—a self-image that is both illusory and harmful.

Freedom is admittedly the simpler value of this pair, for it is easier to formulate and to attain. Equality is more complex, requiring collective action to balance various social components. But simplicity alone should not suggest that a freedom-maximizing society is necessarily the best one, nor that its members will necessarily lead fulfilled lives. Neither should it suggest that a freedom-maximizing society, as it attempts to proceed without deliberate efforts to foster community, will necessarily prove durable. An ongoing and vibrant democratic society needs a balance of liberty and equality, and maintaining that balance has proven to be difficult. I will begin my consideration of these two elements of democracy from the side of liberty.

A certain picture of "natural" human existence—well captured in such expressions as *bellum omnia contra omnes* and *homo homini lupus*—presents it as a battle of all against all, where we treat each other as we think wolves would. Into this battle steps the state as the agent of pacification. The formerly defenseless individuals, in their new role as protected citizens, welcome the suspension of hostilities. They then yield to the state some of their natural rights—for example, private revenge and private warfare—to secure their other rights. As John Locke writes, "The great and *chief end* therefore, of Mens uniting into Commonwealths, and putting themselves under Government, *is the Preservation of their Property,*" which he defines as "their Lives, Liberties and Estates."[1] They unite for the purpose of being left alone, secure in the natural rights that they previously could not defend. They then use the imposed armistice to get about what they take to be the real business of living: advancing the private material well-being of themselves and their families.

This picture is, of course, not historically accurate; but it presents, in a compelling fashion, a rationale for a specific and limited role for government in society. In one form or another this picture has provided the foundation for the efforts of many thinkers over the last few centuries to reduce the role of government in society to internal and external peacekeeping. In the view of these thinkers, since government is essentially repressive in nature, we must be careful not to forget the difference between the government's interests and goals and our own. The goal of these thinkers' efforts has been to minimize restraints and thereby maximize individual freedom. Friedrich A. Hayek asserts that "the whole of this modern period of European history" has demonstrated a process of "freeing the individual from the ties which had bound him to the customary or prescribed ways in the pursuit of his ordinary activities."[2] Rights related to what a person did to earn a living, where that person lived and with whom, how that person dressed, with whom that person could trade and what could be traded, whether interest could be charged for money lending, whether the accumulation of personal wealth was a fit human goal, and so on, were all gained as units of individuals' freedom from the will of others. This increased capacity to act without obstruction by others was, and is, a felt value, a human good.

A fundamental question to be kept in mind when considering this position is whether this position offers the goal of increased individual freedom as a means for reaching a fulfilled life or as human fulfillment itself. Historically, as John Dewey recognized, there has been "a virtual identification of freedom with the very state of being an individual; and the extent of freedom that existed was taken to be the measure of the degree in which individuality was realized" (LW 13:102). The reason for the close fit between freedom as human fulfillment and freedom as a means to human fulfillment is the close connection between economic activity and the core of the human self presented in much of the modern freedom tradition.

Adam Smith's work is a good place to start. His view of human nature contains as an essential element "a naturall disposition" or "a certain propensity . . . to truck, barter, and exchange one thing for another."[3] Another is the desire to prosper: "A man must be perfectly crazy who, where there is tolerable security, does not employ all the stock which he commands . . . in procuring either present enjoyment or future profit."[4] Since we naturally want opulence, and since "it is the division of labour which encreases the opulence of a country,"[5] by making its exchangeable manufactured surpluses cheaper, the division of labor—in spite of its admitted costs[6]—is adopted as the rational method of industrial organization. Life is, for Smith, a private matter of attempting to advance in material well-being. It is an arduous battle against an unforgiving nature and shrewd human competitors. This competitive effort to prosper—to produce better and more cheaply, to trade smarter and more widely—may leave little time for the activities of the citizen; but, since citizenship is an accidental aspect of human living, little is lost.

This apolitical stance was acceptable to Smith because of his belief that we do not create a common good directly by political means. He assumed rather that, with freedom, the workings of the economic system would themselves produce the common good. Beyond the efforts of government to establish a peaceful field for economic activity, no further governmental efforts were necessary—or even desirable. Individual effort would indirectly advance the common good: "the study of his own advantage naturally, or rather necessarily leads him to prefer that employment [for his capital] which is most advantageous to the society."[7] Not all are as sanguine as Smith. In the view of Carl Becker, this freedom approach to economic activity thus reconciled the conflict between the average middle-class individual's selfish and altruistic impulses "by assuring him that he could best love God and his neighbor by doing as he liked."[8] As James Hayden Tufts concludes, "Adam Smith's social philosophy seemed to emancipate economic management from moral responsibility." As he puts it, "If the very nature of things were such as to ensure that private wealth necessarily made for public good, what need for further concern?"[9]

Since individuals cannot know all the consequences of their activities, it would indeed be comforting if they knew in advance that what they did to make money would turn out to be socially beneficial. Assured of this positive outcome through the workings of an "invisible hand," they could safely focus solely upon increasing freedom for individuals engaged in economic interactions. Or, as Tufts put it after the Crash of 1929, "the airship would automatically steer itself and land its passengers in safety at the desired haven of prosperity" so that "the pilot in charge need think only of maintaining full speed ahead."[10] But, in spite of the doubtings of Becker and Tufts and others, the emphasis upon market freedom has remained powerful.

William Graham Sumner, writing a century ago but in a tone very much prevalent today, stresses the importance of recognizing a correlation between market freedom and social progress, on the one hand, and governmental action and social stagnation, on the other: "We cannot go outside of this alternative: liberty, inequality, survival of the fittest; not-liberty, equality, survival of the unfittest. The former carries society forward and favors all its best members; the latter carries society downwards and favors all its worst members."[11] There are those who would deny this harsh reality, Sumner continues—demagogues who would attempt to go against the natural order. But, if they are allowed to do so, others will lose—in Sumner's terms, the "Forgotten Man," "the simple, honest laborer," "the victim of the reformer, social speculator and philanthropist." It is this hard-working and potentially productive laborer who is "weighted down with the cost and burden of the schemes for making everybody happy, with the cost of public beneficence, with the support of all the loafers, with the loss of all the economic quackery, with the cost of all the jobs." To protect "the forgotten man" and to protect social progress it is ever important that we emphasize liberty. "The institutions of civil liberty leave each man to run his career in life in his own way," Sumner continues, "only guaranteeing to him that whatever he does in the way of industry, economy, prudence, sound judgment, etc., shall redound to his own welfare and shall not be diverted to someone else's benefit."[12]

Our picture of this conception of the role of freedom in human existence is about finished: the individual, who naturally seeks material prosperity, when freed to pursue his or her own economic interests, creates personal well-being and wealth. The interference of government with the individual pursuit of wealth—whether it involves plunder by governmental agents themselves or simply a misguided attempt to enforce an egalitarian conception of justice—only undermines the advancement of the common good. Political activity itself is then rendered artificial; if not corrupt, it is certainly unnecessary. Freedom in the marketplace will create the material common good that people naturally desire.

There are other thinkers whose emphasis upon liberty, although equally powerful, is different—demonstrating that even without an emphasis upon economic prosperity, it is still possible to have a vision of human life that makes freedom primary. Perhaps the most powerful formulation of this position in the American tradition is to be found in the writings of Henry David Thoreau, whose sense of fulfillment is just as centrally related to freedom from interference as that of the capitalists whose values he rejects.[13] Thoreau's suggestion for dealing with the "lives of quiet desperation" thought to be forced upon people who can see "no choice left" is to *wake up*. "Moral reform," he writes, "is the effort to throw off sleep." Human unhappiness comes from our half-dozing acceptance of regimentation, from our semiconscious forfeiture of freedom. We wander around as if trapped, taking our cues from other members of the crowd who are wandering just as aimlessly as we are. If each person were to wake up and to listen carefully to his or her own "drummer" and "step to the music . . . however measured or far away,"[14] there would be more happiness.

Attaining personal happiness and fulfillment is thus, for Thoreau, an individual affair, involving self-discovery and self-knowledge, and requiring action free from interference, especially interference by society. Left to their own devices, individuals can more readily heed Thoreau's call to "simplify, simplify," and to avoid all but "the essential facts of life." This need to eliminate complexity is often unrecognized by those who get swept up in the socially driven quest for wealth, for example, the farmer who, in "endeavoring to solve the problem of a livelihood," adopts "a formula more complicated than the problem itself." "To get his shoestrings," Thoreau remarks, "he speculates in herds of cattle."[15] When individuals are freed from such unnecessary complexity by committing themselves to a life shorn of unnecessary wants, they will be able to search for and attain fulfillment.

However sharply Thoreau differs from the supporters of capitalism on the issue of the necessity of economic progress and the naturalness or rationality of the goal of economic prosperity, it is clear that he agrees with them fully on another topic: the apolitical nature of human fulfillment. Collective action is seldom good. "There is but little virtue," he writes, "in the action of masses of men." The majority get their way "because they are physically the strongest, . . . not because they are most likely to be in the right." Human fulfillment is thus not to be sought in cooperative political activities. Democratic government itself, as the tool of the majority, is at best a necessary evil; its laws and decrees are of dubious moral worth. "It is not desirable to cultivate a respect for the law, so much as for the right," he notes. "The only obligation which I have a right to assume, is to do at any time what I think right." Rising above the morass of mass politics is, for Thoreau, the moral insight of individual conscience. "Any man knows when he is justified," he writes, "and all the wits in the world cannot enlighten him on that point."[16] Similarly, anyone who has been able to remain free from the actions and the prejudices of society knows when it has entered upon the wrong course.

When the political situation becomes so bad that individuals can no longer tolerate the evil being carried out in their names, they must take action, Thoreau writes, to "effectually withdraw their support, both in person and property, from the government." Acting "to withdraw and stand aloof from" the state may mean at times only a disengagement from its actions. "It is not a man's duty, as a matter of course, to devote himself to the eradication of any, even the most enormous wrong . . . but it is his duty, at least, to wash his hands of it, and, if he gives it no thought longer, not to give it practically his support." At other times, it is necessary to do more than to remain personally untouched by social evil—it is necessary to stop it. In such cases, Thoreau advises individuals to "break the law. Let your life be a counter friction to stop the machine."[17] I am not concerned here with the question of how we might tell one class of cases from the other—a question that Thoreau answers, at least formally, with his criterion of individual conscience—but to see clearly that even when political events are disastrously wrong, Thoreau does not call us to the ongoing task of constructive citizenship. Our job ends with the end of the evil.

Both of these viewpoints, the capitalists' and Thoreau's, as fundamentally different as they are in some ways, present day-to-day political activity as something on a par with shopping or entertainment seeking. Human fulfillment does not have, in either view, a necessary political component; it requires no ongoing participation in the life of the group. Individuals do not need to grow through political interaction with others. Both of these versions of human fulfillment are based upon the belief that, as Dewey writes, "individuals have such a native or original endowment of rights, powers and wants that all that is required on the side of institutions and laws is to eliminate the obstructions they offer to the 'free' play of the natural equipment of individuals" (LW 3:100). Freedom and fulfillment go hand in hand. Consequently, we have no need to work together to attempt to create a common good—since such a good, by its very nature, cannot be created. All that can be done by society is to foster liberty.

As Herbert Hoover writes, "The primary issue of humanity and all government" is "the issue of human liberty." Freed from interference, left alone by government to make their own way, individuals will prosper and live happy lives. Hoover continues, "Liberty conceives that the mind and spirit of men can be free only if the individual is free to choose his own calling, to develop his talents, to win and to keep a home sacred from intrusion, to rear children in ordered security. It holds he must be free to earn, to spend, to save, to accumulate property that may give protection in old age and to loved ones."[18] Such rights, all private rights, are part of a conception of fulfillment based in freedom.

II

It will be of value at this point to contrast the sense of individualism and human fulfillment that we have just seen with another, offered a decade later by David E. Lilienthal of the Tennessee Valley Authority: A person "wants to feel that he is important. He wants to be able not only to express his opinion freely, but to know that it carries some weight; to know that there are some things that he decides, or has a part in deciding, and that he is a needed and useful part of something far bigger than he is. This hankering to be an *individual* is probably greater today than ever before."[19] I present this radically different sense of the term *individual* not because I am convinced that this latter view, to which I am admittedly partial, should completely replace the former. I present it, rather, to demonstrate that the narrow sense of individuality that we have just been considering is not the final word on human individuality and fulfillment. I have no problem recognizing the value contained in the negative conception of liberty, the value of what Friedrich A. Hayek calls "the absence of restraint and constraint"[20] in our lives so that we may do as we prefer. My concern is, rather, to assess whether the negative conception of liberty is satisfactory with regard to three interrelated issues: the theory of human nature that it is built upon, the development of rights, and the building of permanent community. In each case, I think that it is not.

The first problem that I see resulting from the negative conception of freedom is that it offers an inadequate analysis of human nature, especially with regard to the essence of, and the necessity for, self-imposed limitations. We have seen some hints of these limitations so far—that we should limit our consumption to build capital for later use or later enjoyment or that we should simplify our lives—but, in both of these cases, the aim of the discipline was individual well-being. What I have in mind, however, is the necessity of our individually imposing discipline on ourselves for the common good. Wendell Berry, for example, writes of the importance of developing a "willingness to limit our desires as well as the scale and kind of technology we use to satisfy them" in order to foster a common good grounded in a sound ecology. "Community discipline," he writes, "imposes upon our personal behavior an ecological question: What is the effect, on our neighbors and on our place in the world, of what we do?" To adequately answer this question we must develop "a responsible relationship to the land" grounded in "a particular knowledge of the life of the *place* one lives in and intends to *continue* to live in."[21] This life of self-imposed discipline is related directly to the common good in ways that neither the capitalist's approach nor Thoreau's, wedded as they are to freedom, could be.

This criticism, it must be emphasized, is not to suggest a lack of discipline on the part of those who adopt the negative understanding of freedom. The problem is rather the focus of the discipline they would impose. Their focus forces them to adopt evaluative standards of global proportions in whose satisfaction the permanent local group plays no part. Contemporary business executives who want to get ahead, for example, must weigh their career choices on their employer's scale, a scale that is often location-neutral. Similarly, true followers of Thoreau will care little for their role in a local group as long as they are satisfied with-the anticipated responses of their ideal others. If we adopt these global standards, our social place will be seen as accidental, and we will not engage in the sorts of serious activities that will develop communal roots. But, Berry writes, "People need more than to understand their obligation to one another and to the earth; they need also the *feeling* of such obligation, and the feeling can come only within the patterns of familiarity."[22] This cultivation of the feeling of relations and obligations is necessarily slow and ongoing. It involves learning and changing and finding success in the group. But, if our sense of success is individual, we will place no value in the development of social roots.

Without such roots, without a social place, it is unlikely that we will develop any conception of a public life or any dedication to the creation and fostering of public institutions. Instead, these things will remain accidental to our sense of fulfillment. If, on the other hand, they are essential to our actual fulfillment, we cannot reach lasting happiness without them. I realize that attempting to *prove* that having a social place is essential to human fulfillment to those who would deny it is foolish, but it is worthwhile to consider the following suggestion of Robert N. Bellah and his colleagues about human nature: "We have never been, and still are not, a collection of private individuals who, except for a conscious contract to create a minimal government, have nothing in common. Our lives make sense in a thousand ways, most of which we are unaware of, because of traditions that are centuries, if not millennia, old. It is these traditions that help us to know that it does make a difference who we are and how we treat one another." These ways in which our lives make sense when approached collectively—for example, through shared memories, ceremonies, group shame, common goals—suggest that a lack of individual happiness cannot be solved individually. As they conclude, "This quest for purely private fulfillment is illusory: it often ends in emptiness instead."[23]

Especially as our quest for private fulfillment is aimed at acquisition, it will necessarily fail. As Dewey writes, much of our discontent with our lives is misinterpreted, seen not as a lack of meaningful connections but as a lack of diversions and conquests. "No one knows how much of the frothy excitement of life, of mania for motion, of fretful discontent, of need for artificial stimulation, is the expression of frantic search for something to fill the void caused by the loosening of the bonds which hold persons together in immediate community of experience" (LW 2:368–69; cf. LW 5:65). We attach ourselves to things and crave excitement to overcome our feelings of personal worthlessness; we seek them as indicators of status, success, and well-being. Without connections to a social and geographical place, we find ourselves unable to tell the difference between wants and needs. Thoreau, of course, saw clearly that such a difference does exist and that our failure to honor it is critical. But he was unable to spell out the distinction—to tell his readers what "the essential facts of life" are—perhaps because he denied them Berry's ecological question about how our actions affect others, and hence denied them a social criterion for distinguishing need from want. We need, it seems, a group focus—we need community discipline—to help us develop self-discipline.

The attempt to attain fulfillment through acquisition moreover must fail, at least for the vast majority of people, because of the central role played in our economic life by what Fred Hirsch calls "positional goods." These goods are positional in the sense that they are "either

(1) scarce in some absolute or socially imposed sense" (for example, great old works of art or university teaching positions) "or (2) subject to congestion or crowding through more extensive use" (for example, suburbs that are spoiled by the influx of urban emigrants rushing to participate in their values). Thus defined, these positional goods are necessarily available only to a minority, or else they diminish in value when many have access to them. And, because of their important role in our lives, we may grow individually wealthier yet fail to improve our life situations unless we move up relative to others. "If everyone stands on tiptoe," Hirsch writes, "no one sees better." The consequence of this need for relative advance is the intensification of "positional competition," the inflation of positional costs and great amounts of frustration for those who expect that material progress will lead to widespread individual happiness. As Hirsch concludes, "To see total economic advance as individual advance writ large is to set up expectations that cannot be fulfilled, ever."[24]

The negative conception of freedom thus provides an inadequate understanding of human nature. A second problem is the inadequate conception of human rights that it offers, especially the processive development of rights. We find ourselves at present amid confusing incongruities of rights. For example, explicit federal constitutional guarantees give us more secure rights in what we do with our firearms than in what we do in our sexual lives. A second example of incongruity is that, because of the lack of specific legislative protections for workers, an employer has the ultimate right to close a factory and eliminate thousands of jobs, although it would be illegal for the same employer in the meantime to eliminate the parking spaces for persons with disabilities in the workers' parking lot. These and other incongruencies might be explained, as proponents of negative freedom seem to do, as moments in the uneven process of the liberation of individuals. Although this liberation is a kind of process, they suggest, the rights involved do not themselves develop: they were all aspects of a prior ideal of individual freedom that are just now coming to be respected by society. But, because these individual rights are "natural," they themselves cannot change although the level of protection that we give them might.

Because these individual rights are natural, they do not expand or recede. Thus, although a natural right might become a *lost* right through a lack of vigilance, it can never become a *former* right. These rights cannot, without diminishing our humanity, be yielded to a new social situation, however dangerous or inappropriate to the life of the community they may have become. The right to have a large family, for example, or the right to own a pollution-generating and resource-wasting vehicle, the right to inherit wealth or to dispose of one's investments without taking into account possible harm to others—all go unquestioned. As natural rights, they must be protected from the interference of the masses and the government. On the other hand, because these rights are grounded in our individual humanity rather than in societal attempts to advance the common good, no new rights ever come into being either. Attempts to create or develop "new freedoms" through social cooperation—using Franklin Delano Roosevelt's list, the right to work "usefully and creatively through the productive years," the right to "adequate food, clothing, shelter and medical care," the right to security "from fear of old age, want, dependency, sickness, unemployment and accident," the right to education "for work, for citizenship and for personal growth and happiness," and so on[25]—are to be dismissed as fraud. As Hayek writes, when "some new freedom [is] promised to the people," the intention is almost always to hide the fact that "liberty as we understand it has been destroyed."[26]

Behind the alternative conception of rights that allows for, and even requires, the expansion and contraction of rights is the belief that human life is a continual encounter with the new. As George Herbert Mead suggests, "The next struggle for liberty, or our liberties, will arise out of some infraction that will not have reference to the definition which we have formulated" of what a human person should be, and, consequently, to our current definition of human liberties. "On the contrary, we will find in all probability that the struggle will lead to a quite different definition from the one with which we started" (SW 159). We might uncover some new possibility of liberty that had so far been overlooked; we might encounter some problem with an accepted aspect of liberty that had gone thus far undetected. Our response, this "different definition" of which Mead writes, is part of the processive development of rights that is a fundamental part of our social history but is overlooked by the static, negative conception of freedom.

A third problem with the negative conception of freedom is that it seems to be politically insecure. Grounded as it is in what Dewey calls "a natural opposition between the individual and organized society" (LW 11:8), the negative conception of liberty seems to offer little hope for the permanent securing of human freedom. On the contrary, if ever fully enacted, the negative conception of liberty promises the centrifugal unwinding of society. Rights are really never secure if they are merely seen as personal claims rather than as prerequisites for effective democratic life—for example, when free speech is seen as just my chance to speak my mind rather than as part of a complex arrangement of give-

and-take in which successful results depend upon the sharing and collective evaluation of information. This is so because, as personal matters—or what Dewey calls "*merely* individual claims" (LW 11:374)—these
rights can be portrayed as endangering the common good. Rights seen
as prerequisites for effective democratic life, on the other hand, cannot.
If all people want is to be left alone to prosper or to discover themselves,
it would seem that the members of society will devote little effort to
building the complex web of shared expectations and responsibilities
necessary for the existence of permanent community. The creation of
a common good requires more than developing a social situation in
which all are left alone to do what they want.

If the rights of individuals are to be secured, there must be secure
community. If they are to reflect the broadest extent of freedom possible
at any given time, there must be an ongoing balancing of interests. And,
if individuals are to attain fulfillment, there must be self-imposed limitations grounded in the common good. All three of these requirements
point to the need for a more adequate conception of freedom, a conception of freedom different from the negative one with which we began.

III

At this point, it is probably a good idea to stop briefly and consider in
a bit more explicit detail what 'freedom' might be. It would also be of
value to attempt to adumbrate some relationship among the various
autonomy words: *freedom, rights, independence, liberty,* and so on. There
is, undeniably, adequate evidence of the interpenetration of these various concepts in our normal discourse and of their individual adaptability. As Carl Becker writes, "The word liberty means nothing until it
is given a specific content, and with a little massage will take any content
you like."[27] This adaptability is no reason for abandoning attempts at
definition however. Rather, it makes our attempts more necessary.

I reject in advance the quest for final definitions—and the consequent
implication of the fundamental abuse of meaning, or what Hayek calls
"the complete perversion of language," leveled against those who do
not adopt the inherited meaning held up as a final definition. Hayek
writes that changing the meanings of words is "a technique employed
consciously or unconsciously to direct the people. Gradually, as this
process continues, the whole language becomes despoiled, and words
become empty shells deprived of any definite meaning, as capable of
denoting one thing as its opposite and used solely for the emotional
associations which still adhere to them."[28] I wish to advocate, on the

contrary, a view that supports development or growth in the meaning of key political concepts. I accept here the Pragmatic view that conceptions of political terms carry limitations from their origins that can and should be overcome. James Hayden Tufts, for example, writes that "good and right stand for nothing which can be exactly defined and envisaged once for all." On the contrary, he continues, these values are symbols for "the progressive ideals and standards of a growing moral life, and [they] are constantly taking on new meaning as man knows more fully his powers and kindles more deeply in sympathetic response to his fellows."[29] When applied to the political context, the point remains the same. Our conceptions of key political notions like liberty have been developed through a series of challenges. As Mead writes, "The contents of our so-called natural rights have always been formulated negatively, with reference to restrictions to be overcome" (SW 159). Inherited formulations are thus at least partially time-bound. With time, and with changes in our social situation, we come to see other aspects of freedom as important. Therefore, as Dewey writes, we need to develop a commitment to the "continuous reconstruction of the ideas of individuality and of liberty, in their intimate connection with changes in social relations" (LW 11:292).

What should the various autonomy terms—as conceptualizations of fundamental human values—mean at present? My own unenforceable views run as follows. *Freedom,* I would suggest, can best be understood as a state of being able to make and act upon choices in all matters of importance. This state obviously requires more than the lack of interference required in the negative conception explored above. *Liberty,* I would suggest, is essentially synonymous with *freedom.*[30] *Rights* I see as individual units of freedom, like the right to vote or the right to consume alcoholic beverages, that are socially defended at any given time (or are at least proposed as being worthy of such a defense, as in the right to work in a smoke-free environment). *Independence* I would use as a political term to describe the collective status of autonomy possessed by a group of individuals who are able to collectively decide their shared fate.

With regard to all these concepts, it seems to me obvious that all the aspects of autonomy—economic, social, political, educational, and so on—are intermeshed, but this question of fullness of freedom remains an open one. Hayek, for example, defends a narrow sense of freedom, declaring that only the *political* aspects of liberty are matters of freedom and that once we move into what he sees as the distinct realm of economics we are concerned not with freedom but with power: "To the great apostles of political freedom the word had meant freedom from coercion, freedom from the arbitrary power of other men, release from ties which left the individual no choice but obedience to the orders of a superior to whom he was attached. The new freedom promised, however, was to be freedom from necessity, release from the compulsion of the circumstances which inevitably limit the range of choice of all of us, although for some very much more than for others."[31] The heart of the distinction between economic and political controls is that the controls that are political in nature result directly "from the arbitrary power of other men" and thus endanger freedom, whereas economic controls—because they result from "impersonal forces" or "nobody's conscious choice" and are "not designed to affect particular people in a particular way"[32]—do not endanger freedom even though they do admittedly result in inequality and differential restraints. The primary social value, for Hayek, is freedom.

The attempt to define freedom requires us to consider at some point the question of the relative importance of freedom and other human goods. Clearly some values fall outside the narrow conception of freedom we have just seen, equality being the primary one, and these values must be advanced in any good society. A society that advanced only freedom—although it is questionable whether it would be a *society* at all—would surely not be a good society. As Tufts writes, in addition to freedom, "cooperation, responsibility, justice, are all of them values which the community must secure."[33] Moreover, a society cannot always advance freedom. Unless we reject in advance such usages as the freedom to sin, to harm, or to make mistakes, we recognize that we must at times constrain freedom. Therefore, it would seem that freedom as a human good is to be advanced, but advanced only within the context of the ongoing life of the democratic community. Freedom is not the primary human good.

I recognize, of course, that members of various societies, including many of our own at present, do not agree here. Individual freedom is often seen as the primary value for a society to advance. Hoover writes, for example, that "democracy is merely the mechanism which individualism invented as a device that would carry on the necessary political work of its social organization."[34] Perhaps this emphasis upon freedom results from the contemporary belief that, as Hayek maintains, "the craving for freedom" is "the strongest of all political motives."[35] Perhaps it results from public confusion brought about by those who have the most to gain from the operation of unrestrained freedom. Or, perhaps it results from a failure on the part of the members of society to distinguish adequately between personal freedom and national independence. In any case, we are now a freedom-focused and, not accidentally, a troubled society. Movement toward a successful and fulfilling democratic society will require a rebalancing of freedom and equality.

IV

A more balanced understanding of democracy can be had by developing a sense of communal liberty, of liberty grounded in community life. "Cooperation," Dewey writes, "is as much a part of the democratic ideal as is personal initiative" (LW 13:78; cf. LW 9:103). This sense of communal liberty aims at "a kind of individual freedom that is general and shared and that has the backing and guidance of socially organized intelligent control" (LW 11:137). This sense of freedom, as a value when rooted in community, is itself based in a social sense of the self and its fulfillment that draws upon Dewey's claim that "shared experience is the greatest of human goods" (LW 1:157).

This social sense of the self views the self neither as something with which a person begins his or her life nor as something that grows from within when the person is uninterfered with. Rather the social approach views the self as something that emerges in the process of social interaction. "Everything which is distinctively human is learned, not native," Dewey writes. "To learn to be human is to develop through the give-and-take of communication an effective sense of being an individually distinctive member of a community" (LW 2:331–32; cf. MSS 135–44). True individuality, in this sense, is a cluster of abilities developed over time, through interaction. Such individuality, he continues, "means initiative, inventiveness, varied resourcefulness, assumption of responsibility in choice of belief and conduct. These are not gifts, but achievements" (MW 12:191), achievements of rooted individuals. And these achievements, it cannot be stressed enough, are social, not private. "No man and no mind was ever emancipated merely by being left alone," Dewey writes. "Liberty is that secure release and fulfillment of personal potentialities which takes place only in rich and manifold association with others" (LW 2:340, 329).

In building social selves, the importance of temporality is central. This means, among other things, that social arrangements, laws, and other institutions, as semipermanent aspects of our social lives, must foster individuality. As Peter T. Manicas writes, "Persons only become human in association with others, but not all associations liberate human powers."[36] As Dewey asserts, institutions are "means and agencies of human welfare and progress. . . . They are means of *creating* individuals" (MW 12:191). Consequently, to view institutions "as enemies of freedom, and all conventions as slaveries, is to deny the only means by which positive freedom in action can be secured" (MW 14:115). This positive freedom is gained by using the possibilities made available by institutions to develop individuals' capacities to draw upon the past and contribute to the future.

Another part of what must be fostered in this temporal understanding of the self is a recognition of the importance of our connection with the future. By our choices we are building a world in which we will never live. We are leaving behind for those who are to come many institutions—patterns of energy production and transportation, of health care and international relations, of education and economic organization—some of them good, some of them bad, all of them our responsibility. As Dewey writes in this regard:

> We who now live are parts of a humanity that extends into the remote past, a humanity that has interacted with nature. The things of civilization we most prize are not of ourselves. They exist by grace of the doings and sufferings of the continuous human community in which we are a link. Ours is the responsibility of conserving, transmitting, rectifying and expanding the heritage of values we have received that those who come after us may receive it more solid and secure, more widely accessible and more generously shared than we have received it (LW 9:57–58).

We must attempt to foster this sense of connection to the members of society who are to come after us as an essential part of our self-understanding.

Still another part of the temporality of the self that we must emphasize is the ongoing processive development of the individual. Our aim at all times must be growth. Freedom, Tufts writes, means the "opportunity to develop powers through the heritage of man's past achievement and the resources of present cooperation."[37] Growing persons are those who use this heritage and these resources to make themselves happier and more useful. This is, Dewey writes, how we ought to approach the various fundamental choices of our lives. What is actually at stake "in any serious deliberation" is "what kind of person one is to become, what sort of self is in the making," and ultimately "what kind of a world" is in the making (MW 14:150). We must ask which alternative in this deliberation would favor growth.

It is important to recognize here that a large component of this growth, and consequently of freedom, is intellectual in nature. Thus Dewey can write that we are free "in the degree in which we act knowing what we are about" (LW 4:199) and that "what men actually cherish under the name of freedom is that power of varied and flexible growth, of change of disposition and character, that springs from intelligent choice" (LW 3:111). "Genuine freedom is intellectual; it rests in the trained *power of thought,* in ability to 'turn things over,' to look at matters deliberately" (LW 8:186). Here too, freedom means more than being left alone: "We take for granted the necessity of special opportunity and prolonged education to secure ability to think in a special calling, like mathematics. But we appear to assume that ability to think effectively in social, political and moral matters is a gift of God, and that the gift operates by a kind of spontaneous combustion" (LW 3:112–13). On the contrary, it is only by sharing our commonly held wisdom that we have any hope of freeing ourselves from the scourges of poverty and disease, from the drudgery of the workplace and the tragedy of the battlefield. The freedom necessary to accomplish these tasks will come only with shared intellectual growth.

Human fulfillment is, in this analysis, to be found in shared experience, in the cooperative search for solutions, in contribution to the common good. "Sooner or later," Mary Parker Follett writes, "every one in a democracy must ask himself, what am I worth to society?"[38] What the individual seeking to be fulfilled wants, Dewey declares, is to participate. For this individual, the democratic ideal "consists in having a responsible share according to capacity in forming and directing the activities of the groups to which one belongs and in participating according to need in the values which the groups sustain." In this way, we can foster "the power to be an individualized self making a distinctive contribution and enjoying in its own way the fruits of association" (LW 2:327–29).

This participation is a community ideal not just because people will be happier thereby but because they can thereby grow through interaction and learn to do an increasingly better job of self-government. With effort we can advance the dual goal that Tufts described as "a progressive social development in which every member of society shall share."[39] By participating in the social life of the neighborhood, congregation, union, and school, individuals can get a better feel for various social problems, develop the ability to evaluate the personalities and plans of others, and make their own contributions. Through the shared process of initiating, discussing, evaluating, choosing, implementing, and reevaluating, we can refine our goals and purposes and test our available means. Participants in face-to-face groups can be creators and re-creators of social life. Attempts at social progress need not be based upon acquiescence to what parties and bureaucracies and hierarchies and leaderships decide.

At times, so much emphasis is placed upon participation that it may seem that the process of democratic interaction is more important than actual success. Dewey writes, for example, that "democracy is the faith that the process of experience is more important than any special result attained," but he offers this comment only in the context of an explicit linkage between the process of democratic interaction ("of consultation, of conference, of persuasion, of discussion") and the likelihood of success through the "formation of public opinion, which in the long-run is self-corrective" (LW 14:229, 227). The point is that, with continued interaction, success remains a possibility. As Paul Goodman suggests, even a serious conflict "is not an obstacle to community . . . *if the give-and-take can continue, if contact can be maintained.*"[40] By exercising our shared responsibility to create human lives for ourselves and others according to rules that we have collectively developed, we can achieve greater levels of democracy and human fulfillment in our society.

Because participating in community life is important to human fulfillment, and because the effective evaluation of our social efforts is important to society's success, we need to reconsider the question of equality. Leaving aside for now questions of economic justice, and concentrating solely on the issues of human fulfillment and political efficacy, it is still possible to argue that in order for citizens to effectively contribute to society according to their ability, the various institutions of society and the powers of various citizens must be in some rough balance. "When the parties involved in any transaction are unequal in status," Dewey writes, "the relationship is likely to be one-sided, and the interests of one party to suffer" (LW 2:274).[41] Thus, rejecting the view that people "are equally free to act if only the same legal arrangements apply equally to all—irrespective of differences in education, in command of capital, and the control of the social environment which is furnished by the institution of property" (LW 3:100; cf. LW 11:360–63), Dewey calls for "effective liberty," which requires "social control of economic forces in the interest of the great mass of individuals" (LW 11:27). In the face of the glaring inequalities of modern life, Tufts writes, if democracy is to be preserved, "government is forced to interfere to preserve liberty."[42] Or, as Dewey puts it, "government should regularly intervene to help equalize conditions between the wealthy and the poor, between the overprivileged and the underprivileged" (LW 11:285).

This call for equality as a means to full social participation rejects as inadequate a sense of equality that would rest solely on equal opportunity. This rejection of the equal opportunity approach is not based so much upon questioning the dubious criteria for certifying that equality of opportunity exists as it is upon questioning the whole project. What the equal opportunity approach holds forth as its goal is an equal chance—or, more restrictedly, equal access to a chance[43]—to succeed at individual goals through personal effort (to hit baseballs, to enter law school, to amass a personal fortune). What is being claimed under an equal participation approach is something else altogether. The equal right to participate fully in the decision-making process of society requires that we have a goal of achieving a greater degree of equality of condition—a more equal level of education and career, of free time and travel and culture, of economic security and future possibilities. Then we could, Dewey writes, embody in our lives "equality and freedom expressed not merely externally and politically but through personal participation in the development of a shared culture" (LW 5:57). Obviously, this kind of equality is something that we do not now have, but it is something for which we should work by reemphasizing the egalitarian aspects of democracy.

At this point we might stop to consider other thinkers who reject the individual sense of the self found in the capitalist tradition and in thinkers like Thoreau but who do not suggest that we attempt to adopt the stance of the communal citizen. For these individuals, of whom Reinhold Niebuhr is perhaps the best known, the kind of full and working community I have suggested is not a realistic possibility. He maintains that the political realm will "to the end of history, be an area where conscience and power meet, where the ethical and coercive factors of human life will interpenetrate and work out their tentative and uneasy compromises."[44] Niebuhr, and others with similar viewpoints,[45] may ultimately be right: the kind of inquiring community that deliberately fosters the development of a common good, which is necessary to make an egalitarian society work, may be impossible to attain. It may be that the good society for which many hope is capable only "of approximation but not of realisation." Perhaps, as Niebuhr claims, the most we can hope for is to create a society "in which there will be enough justice, and in which coercion will be sufficiently non-violent to prevent [humankind's] common enterprise from issuing into complete disaster."[46]

On the other hand—and this is the Pragmatic position that I am advocating—Niebuhr and the others may be wrong. Community may be possible. In any case, two aspects of their "realistic" position deserve special consideration. The first is that we must recognize explicitly that the answer is not yet in and that what we assume to be possible, and impossible, will influence our ongoing social practice and our ultimate social success. If we convince ourselves in advance that full community is impossible and aim only at "approximation," we are certain to be satisfied sooner than we should be. Second, if we overlook Niebuhr's pessimistic analysis of our social reality, we see that his conclusion—

that in a good society there must be some limit to controls and some minimal level of economic justice—is very similar to the one I am suggesting: no democracy can long succeed unless it advances both freedom and equality.

Although my aim in this chapter has been to challenge the primacy of liberty as a social value, I do not advocate a society based solely on equality. That society would be no better than one that was devoted only to liberty. Drawing heavily upon the ideas of Pragmatic social thought, I have suggested instead that a successful democracy can exist only if it can maintain the intricate balance between equality and liberty, only if freedom and community are integrated. Although other qualities of a good society, such as general civility and procedural justice, are politically important, I do not see them as *democratic* values. The vital balance between liberty and equality cannot be maintained unless the members of society make an ongoing commitment to participate in social life. This commitment has always been important. It is particularly necessary now.

7

Optimism, Meliorism, Faith

Americans have long whistled an optimistic tune. Aside from the occasional self-styled "realist," whose assessment of our situation has been more negative, Americans have long acted with the conviction that it was a manageable task to make "the face of nature smile"—whether in the narrow agricultural sense of nature that Crèvecoeur here intended or in a much broader sense of nature as the place where we and our children live our lives. While it was admitted that our advancement surely could be "impeded or accelerated by human will and effort," Arthur A. Ekirch notes, it was generally believed that "progress was indeed certain."[1]

From the start, in the eyes of Europeans and Americans alike, America was a new land full of opportunity. It was a land that drew hopeful individuals, individuals possessed by what John E. Smith has called "the belief in the lure, the power and the promise of the *future*." And, for the most part, the promise came true. Americans were, in a fundamental sense, a people weaned on what Henry F. May has called "the continuing experience of triumph," and they came to expect that this process of advancement would continue. Progress was not a theory or an abstract possibility; it was a fact, and this fact of progress gave rise to optimism.[2]

One key to explaining Americans' traditional optimism has been the possibility of progress inherent in the open frontier of the West. As long as we Americans could draw upon free land—free at least in white eyes—beyond the places of current conflict, we could expect what Frederick Jackson Turner called the "perennial rebirth" of the frontier. On the one hand, this rebirth was economic: Americans believed that by owning their own land they could escape from the financial dependence they had known back East. On the other hand, it was a social rebirth: building new communities meant opportunities to rise to full equality through active participation in self-government. As Turner wrote of this dual rebirth: "These free lands promoted individualism, economic equality, freedom to rise, democracy. Men would not accept inferior wages and a permanent position of social subordination when this promised land of freedom and equality was theirs for the taking. . . . In a word, then, free lands meant free opportunities."[3] There was, as long as the open frontier lasted, a belief in the opportunity to start over; even those who did not go West held in the back of their minds the possibility of leaving should their situations become unacceptable. Thus for East and West, the frontier contributed to American optimism.

We recognize, of course, that the open frontier was not the whole story of American optimism. For one thing, the reality of the situation on the frontier and in the urban centers was far more complex than Turner's analysis suggested.[4] Second, even after we realized that the frontier had closed and that, in the words of Franklin Delano Roosevelt, "opportunity would no longer be equal" since the "safety valve" of the "Western prairie" was gone, still the hopefulness remained. Through positive efforts by the government and through legislation featuring what he called "the new terms of the old social contract," Roosevelt maintained that we could accomplish by deliberate political means what the frontier had accomplished by happy accident. It would not be easy, of course; but, with effort, it would be possible. In spite of the sea of social problems that had risen and was to carry him to national office, in spite of the clear evidence of a society then nearing collapse, Roosevelt maintained that "failure is not an American habit."[5] And he continued to believe, as did many others, that we could solve our social problems if we but applied to them the spirit that had led to scientific progress.

With Lester Frank Ward, Americans refused to admit "that man shall ultimately obtain the dominion of the whole world except himself." Their hope for social reform was a part of the long tradition in Western philosophy—sometimes rationalist, sometimes romantic, sometimes evolutionary—that asserted, in the words of Clarke A. Chambers, that "through an understanding of the laws of society, men could establish direction over the course of history and could thus mold the future to fulfill their own needs and desires." Bringing this about, moreover, required no great social upheaval but, as Walter E. Weyl wrote, "simply a quicker turn of the wheel *in the direction in which the wheel is already turning*." Continued progress through satisfactory social reforms was within our capabilities; and, therefore, even in times of trouble and strife we could safely remain optimistic.[6]

The writings of many Americans evinced this belief that circumstances would work themselves out. As we read, sometimes we see the extravagant: "The irresistible tendency of the human race," writes George Bancroft, is "to advancement. . . . Humanity has always been on the advance." Sometimes a writer shows a better recognition of the costs to be incurred, such as Carl Sandburg:

> The learning and blundering people will live on.
> They will be tricked and sold and again sold
> And go back to the nourishing earth for rootholds,
> The people so peculiar in renewal and comeback,
> You can't laugh off their capacity to take it.

But both cases, as well as many others, demonstrate the optimistic belief of Americans that over time things will work out. "Time is ample" is how Walt Whitman put it.[7]

We might wish to stop here and challenge this optimism, reminding ourselves of the failures, the victims, the suffering, and the waste. When we recall these costs, we gain a sense of the meaning of the following comment by Thomas Vernor Smith: "Finding themselves in a land where countless situations baffled control, early Americans, like the early Hebrews, converted the scarcity and want of actual fact into the milk and honey of gratifying imagination." This conversion, as we have seen, continued beyond the early Americans, and there have been others who have pointed to it. George Santayana, for example, called American optimism "a thin disguise for despair," and Randolph Bourne saw it in a similar fashion: "Optimism is often compensatory, and the optimistic mood in American thought may mean merely that American life is too terrible to face."[8]

Although this aspect of the topic of optimism must remain in the back of our minds, my main purpose in this chapter is to consider just the role of optimism, broadly conceived, in social action. We have been examining Pragmatic social thought, especially the work of John Dewey and George Herbert Mead, with an emphasis upon intelligence and method. An essential element of their view on social reconstruction has to do with the nature of social possibilities. Behind all of their social and political writings are to be found beliefs that the cooperative efforts of active and concerned citizens could shape our somewhat open future toward higher levels of social well-being and that commitment to social action beyond assured success is both necessary and justifiable.

II

Any consideration of optimism in American philosophical thought must begin with Ralph Waldo Emerson. This is true not only because his work is so thoroughly and strenuously optimistic but also because he so clearly exposes the strands of a full optimism against which we can measure other thinkers. Emerson tells us that even though the natural world is "rough and surly," it is made to serve "the dominion of man." Further, "no statement of the Universe can have any soundness which does not admit its ascending effort." Indeed, "melioration is the law. The cruelest foe is a masked benefactor."⁹ Underlying this belief in melioration is a doctrine that Emerson calls "the law of Compensation": "For every thing you have missed, you have gained something else; and for every thing you gain, you lose something." Although this law of compensation should be read both ways—to lose is to gain, and vice versa—many readers of this law, and here Emerson must be included, downplay the latter half. For Emerson the optimist, the meliorative side of compensation is primary: "Nature turns all malfeasance to good"; and, what is more, "the sentiment of Right . . . is the voice of the universe." With this understanding of how wrongs will be righted, Emerson can claim still further that "honest service cannot come to loss. If you serve an ungrateful master, serve him the more. Put God in your debt."¹⁰

In these passages on compensation, we see the sweeping optimism of Emerson. He begins with a doctrine of balance that might serve anyone well as a reminder of the frailty of human existence and the folly of self-congratulation. But he then moves to a belief in a system of reality that balances goods and evils and, further, to a doctrine that all evils will be made good. Finally, he arrives at the position that we may lay passive and await redemption from our ills. In fact, as the following passage shows, Emerson believes that we should be passive: "there is no need of struggles, convulsions, and despairs, of the wringing of the hands and the gnashing of the teeth. . . . we miscreate our own evils. We interfere with the optimism of nature."¹¹

Present in these revealing passages are two key assumptions that comprise the heart of Emerson's optimism. The first is his belief that nature (or reality, or God) is on our side, that human well-being is the highest priority of the cosmic system of which we are a part. The second key assumption is that we may, and even should, remain passive in the face of what appear to be ills since, in any system that holds human well-being primary, such ills can be only apparent. Arising out of these assumptions is a full sense of optimism that few would find defensible.

To forego the second assumption and make only the first—that nature is on our side—would constitute a sense of optimism more compatible with the history of the American experience that we have briefly explored. I suspect that this belief that nature is on our side is accepted as well by many contemporary Americans who believe that so-called controlled growth without limit is possible or that the environment can heal itself over time regardless of the type or level of damage we do to it.

But what of individuals who reject both of these assumptions? Can we still talk about the optimism of thinkers when they assert openly that nature has no care for us and that even with our best efforts we may fail to overcome the ills we face? Certainly we cannot call such thinkers optimistic in the absolute sense that we have just been examining. Once they have surrendered the metaphysical security of nature's concern for our well-being, absolute optimism is impossible. But another, more relative sense of optimism is possible. A thinker can be more or less optimistic in this more relative sense, independent of beliefs about the place of human well-being in nature, solely on the grounds of anticipating success in our social actions. In what is to follow, I shall be considering optimism in this second, relative sense.

The work of Pragmatic social thinkers like Dewey and Mead is often presented as being excessively optimistic in terms of this relative sense of optimism. Certainly, we can find in Dewey instances of a kind of prima facie optimism—expectations that do not seem to be fully justified by the facts of our situation. Dewey believed, for example, that with the growth in the use of the scientific method a new intellectual era was dawning, an era that would have profound effects on all of human life.[12] He believed that in our movements toward a highly cooperative community, there are "no insuperable obstacles, given the intelligent will for its realization" (MW 9:326). We can be reasonably confident that no permanent regress will befall us: "If we want [progress], we can have it, if we are willing to pay the price in effort, especially in effort of intelligence." These changes had not happened as yet, but the conditions for their institution were "at hand" (MW 10:237). We could be confident in the future application of our method because of what it "has already accomplished in subduing to potential human use the energies of physical nature" (LW 11:64). Science, although "still in its babyhood" (LW 15:161; cf. LW 16:375–79), would enable us to address our problems effectively. Given sufficient time and adequate developments in education and communication, the "self-correcting nature of scientific inquiry" (LW 12:483) would be integrated within the processive development of public opinion, "which in the long run is self-corrective" (LW 14:227). All this would result, finally, in a more intelligent community. In fact, by making our political action a cooperative and educational process, even our mistakes can be seen as learning experiences; apparent catastrophes like the Great Depression become "a small price to pay" (LW 6:63)[13] if they waken us to the danger of continued drift.

Similarly, we can find numerous instances of prima facie optimism in the works of Mead. He believed, as we have seen above, that humankind was increasingly "at home" in the world (SW 264) because humans had "gradually become aware of the method of meeting [their] problems" (PA 508). Further, we can safely expect to move onward without predetermined long-range goals, relying upon intelligent adjustments as we go.[14] Mead believed, too, that the world of nature was increasingly submitting to rational organization through our developing control of the environment.[15] He saw, in addition, the increasing control of social life through the inclusion of instruments of rational change within our governmental framework (cf. SW 150–70). Moreover, he tells us that we can safely expect a day when the disrupting influences of individuals and groups against the common good will be minimized,[16] when cultures will understand each other more fully (cf. PA 510–11), and when the human community will no longer permit its members to endure the kind of suffering that it has in the past.[17]

Neither Dewey nor Mead thought that this new world would be established easily or maintained without cost. Throughout Pragmatic social thought we find the view that the work of establishing and maintaining democratic community must be rooted in the cooperative use of intelligence and that it will require the ongoing reconstruction of our educational, industrial, and political systems both to create higher levels of shared interests and to foster clearer recognition of these interests among the citizenry. "If we can control the means we become responsible for the new ends which they enable us to form," Mead writes, yet "we have come far short of accepting that responsibility."[18] Dewey notes in a similar mood, "To foresee consequences of existing conditions is to surrender neutrality and drift; it is to take sides in behalf of the consequences that are preferred" (LW 5:109–10).

One question of importance for us as scholars and citizens is to determine the function of optimistic beliefs in social existence, not only in the context of Pragmatic social thought but also in our own. There are those who tell us that optimistic beliefs are a delusion based upon the denial of the most obvious kinds of evidence. Should we act on this delusion of cooperative intelligence, they warn, we will waste our lives in futile commitment. What is worse, they maintain, is that we will become dupes of the malevolent, used for purposes that we do not support through our performance of actions that we do not fully understand. Others, the Social Pragmatists among them, are of a different opinion. For them, this type of optimism is a necessary element in social existence because it underlies the commitment we must share to extend ourselves for eventual community success.

III

For many today, the buoyancy of this Pragmatic stance seems no longer adequate. It is a philosophy that was, in the words of May Brodbeck, "based on a wish and a hope," a philosophy that "could not long endure—not even in America."[19] For some, the confidence that we could do what we set our minds to do, which once seemed so eminently sensible, vanished, as Asher Moore notes, "in the concentration camps and undergrounds of Hitler's Europe."[20] For others, this confidence vanished earlier, in the trenches of the Western Front, or later, in the jungles of Southeast Asia; vanished in the recognition of the fragility of our restraints on nuclear holocaust, or in our apparent need to make choices that trade off the quality of our children's environment for funds to pay their dental bills; vanished in the realization that our goals of racial and sexual equality have costs elsewhere, or that a government powerful enough to attain our desired goals will acquire goals of its own. They no longer look at new problems as challenges to be overcome in the reconstructive process of living. They are tired of solving problems and afraid that the next time we might fail. Such individuals are often drawn to the work of thinkers other than the Pragmatists—thinkers who believe that human cooperation can never overcome what they see as our inbred fundamental selfishness or that human intelligence cannot hope to keep pace with the increasing complexity of our social existence.

Those who see humans as fundamentally selfish rather than cooperative claim that thinkers like Dewey and Mead fail to understand and take account of, as Paul E. Pfuetze writes, "the stark reality of moral evil in men and societies." This evil enables people to lie to themselves about their aims and motives and to use power for their own aggrandizement. Reinhold Niebuhr was perhaps the most influential exponent of this view. For Niebuhr, the Pragmatic understanding overlooks "the complexities of human behavior" that result from conflicts between the objectives of reason and "those of the total body of impulse, rationally unified but bent upon more immediate goals than those which man's highest reason envisages." As a result, "there are definite limits in the capacity of ordinary mortals" to transcend their own self-interest.[21]

Pragmatic social thinkers like Dewey and Mead deny that selfishness poses such limitations, or they at least place them differently than thinkers like Niebuhr do because they believe that individuals can learn to act with a high degree of impartiality. In fact, one way to approach Pragmatic social thought is to see it as the attempt to attain social harmony through heightening impartiality. As Mead tells us, the solution to social ills results from the adoption, on the part of members of society, of the stance of the other and the consequent creation of "a larger whole in terms of which the social conflicts that necessitate the reconstruction of the given society are harmonized or reconciled, and by reference to which, accordingly, these conflicts can be solved or eliminated" (MSS 308–9; cf. Dewey, LW 13:115). For Niebuhr, on the other hand, this claim is seriously mistaken because "the worst injustices and conflicts of history arise from these very claims of impartiality."[22] We find then in Niebuhr, and in others of like mind, the condemnation of Dewey and Mead's approach to social action through a method grounded in impartial cooperation as naive and utopian, and eventually counterproductive.

The other challenge to a method of cooperative intelligence in social action is rooted in the belief that humans, although not necessarily too selfish to follow such a method, are simply not intelligent enough to make it work. Critics of this persuasion attack the "stubborn confidence" of individuals like Dewey and Mead in human rationality as a means of overcoming social problems. Sometimes this criticism is wildly overstated and inaccurate, as when it attributes to thinkers like Dewey and Mead an "unqualified trust in intelligence as the power in man which can guide him toward the resolution of any problem." At other times this criticism seems to be a front for a return to a religious dependence, as when it attacks "an unrealistic over-confidence in man's unaided powers."[23] But the various strands seem to amount to the same thing: human intelligence is not enough to solve our problems.

Perhaps the clearest expression of this criticism is in the writings of Joseph Wood Krutch, who announced that "man's ingenuity has outrun his intelligence."[24] The basis of this distinction between ingenuity and intelligence is the often-encountered belief in the existence of two fundamentally distinct realms of reality—using Niebuhr's terms, "the realm of history" and "the realm of nature"—and the further belief that, because science is not fully applicable to the realm of history, to hope for a scientific resolution of human problems is to hope in vain.[25] As another commentator writes, it is "utopian" to believe that "because science has had considerable success in dealing with one type of problem, it must be successful in dealing with problems of an altogether different type."[26] Rather than science offering answers to our problems, science, through its trespass into "the realm of history," has in fact caused, and is continuing to cause, more and worse problems than it can ever hope to remedy.

For these two reasons, then, the method of cooperative intelligence in such thinkers as Dewey and Mead has been rejected by many. On the one hand, there is the belief that people are fundamentally selfish— in some sense evil or "sinful" (LW 16:416)—and that consequently to expect of them a high degree of concern and care for their neighbors is utopian. On the other hand, there is the belief that the veneer of human intelligence is a thin one and that human ingenuity will continue to cause more problems than it will solve until and unless it is curtailed (see LW 16:416). In combination, these two criticisms amount to the condemnation of the social method of cooperative intelligence as inadequate to the task of solving our problems and the dismissal of the optimistic hopefulness found in Pragmatic social thought as a delusion.

IV

So far, we have been concentrating baldly upon Dewey and Mead's estimates of future possibilities, and it is time to begin considering more closely the factors that condition these estimates. Under what circumstances do Dewey and Mead expect success? To explore these circumstances is not to attempt to deny their prima facie optimism. It is simply to demonstrate the context of their thinking. When this context is more clear, we shall see that it is a caricature to maintain that the proponents of Pragmatic social thought were confident of certain success or that they saw in human beings only good. Dewey and Mead are almost always explicitly cautious in their claims about human amiability and possible future successes. The only categorical claim that they make repeatedly is that our attempts to bring about improvement are worthwhile.

Considering the two complaints of selfishness and stupidity in reverse order, we can begin with the criticism that Dewey and Mead are overly confident about human intelligence as a means to solve our problems. Here the fact is that they recognized, and repeatedly pointed out, the inherent limits on our problem-solving abilities. Intelligence is not magic, and the scientific method offers no guarantees. Mead notes that he is "not so silly as to suppose that, if we were simply willing to be intelligent, we could in the immediate future solve" our fundamental social problems (PA 490). "All action," Dewey writes, "is an invasion of the future, of the unknown." Consequently all action leads to unexpected results. "Men always build better or worse than they know"

(MW 14:10, 143). Even when we make use of the best scientific information and techniques available, results will be ambiguous because, as Dewey notes, "There is probably no case in which the good achieved by the intervention of science has not been offset by some evil" (LW 16:373; cf. 365) that will emerge in subsequent experience and will have to be addressed.

Intelligence is not the ability to solve matters once and for all. It is, rather, the process of ongoing adjustment to novel situations. Moreover, with many sorts of problems "adaptation" is impossible, and our "adjustment" is limited to "accommodation" (LW 9:12). And, because living is not a "research problem [that] may be left because of our inability to find a satisfactory hypothesis" (SW 257), we often find ourselves making inadequate and painful compromises. We know that new struggles and new failures are inevitable because "it is certain that problems will recur in the future in a new form or on a different plane" (MW 14:197). Consequently, "when all is said and done, the fundamentally hazardous character of the world is not seriously modified, much less eliminated." The world remains, in Dewey's words, a "precarious and perilous" place (LW 1:45, 42).

When we turn to the question of human selfishness, we see that for neither Dewey nor Mead are we totally self-transparent. Thus, even though they do not see humans as the egoists of Niebuhr's portrayal, neither do they see the human products of evolution as "children of light" as Niebuhr claims they do. Mead believes that much of what he calls the "primal stuff of which we are made up" is not "under our direct control" (SW 358). As Dewey recognizes, the human being "is naturally or primarily an irrational creature" (MW 13:247; cf. MW 11:107–11). "Impulse and habit, not thought, are the primary determinants of conduct" (MW 14:153). The meaning of these facts, however, is not what it is for the critics: namely, that individuals, regardless of how civilized they may seem, have an impenetrable, asocial core. For Dewey and Mead, this "irrational" core is not impenetrable. This is so because even if, as Dewey writes, "conduct proceeds from conditions which are largely out of focal attention," still "the underlying and generative conditions of concrete behavior are social as well as organic." In fact, they are "much more social than organic as far as the manifestation of *differential* wants, purposes and methods of operation is concerned" (LW 2:299). Therefore, through social action it is possible to shape and channel individual conduct. As Mead writes, because we have "no direct control over our loves and our hates," we must rely upon our "social organization" (SW 359, 369). From the Pragmatic perspective, as Dewey writes, "Native human nature supplies the raw materials, but custom furnishes the machinery and the designs" (MW 14:78). It is through the reconstruction of the customs and institutions that many hold to be human nature that selfishness can be addressed.

Furthermore, even if Dewey and Mead maintain that these institutions, and ultimately the scientific method, are in some sense self-correcting—that is, that they help to bring to light, over time, mistakes and problems that were previously overlooked—both recognize that they can never become self-directing. The scientific method cannot tell us what the problems are and what will count as solutions: individuals must bring their own perspectives to bear on the emerging situation. Consequently our efforts must always be directed by individuals. We must therefore continue to make of our impulsive and habitual selves inquirers who have what Dewey calls "the social sensitiveness" to recognize and address the significant problems and issues of the present and future (MW 12:165). As he writes, it is just false to maintain that "facts are just there and need only to be observed accurately and be assembled in sufficient number to warrant generalizations" (LW 12:491). It is human creativity and insight that allows us to recognize the problems and construct the hypotheses that lead to their solutions. Simply put, "science itself is an instrument which is indifferent to the external uses to which it is put" (LW 6:55), and therefore success can never be guaranteed.

In light of this, we surely cannot be blindly optimistic. We cannot claim, Dewey writes, "that intelligence will ever dominate the course of events," nor "that it will save [us] from ruin and destruction" (LW 1:325–26). Dewey offers us this reminder because he believes that any such conclusion leads us away from the ever-necessary task of reconstruction to complacency and to a confusion of "rapidity of change with advance" (MW 10:234–35). It is necessary to have a constant search for answers because the necessary social understanding will not be created "unless we strive for it" (LW 9:51). Nevertheless, though we cannot be blindly optimistic, on the other hand, we should not be pessimistic either. How much success we will have if we try our best remains to be seen. We cannot be sure just how far the method of intelligence will get us, but Dewey and Mead assume that it will get us farther than any other method. As Dewey writes, the claim that "intelligence is a better method than its alternatives, authority, imitation, caprice and ignorance, prejudice and passion, is hardly an excessive claim" (LW 1:326). Even if we are not certain that it will work, the fostering of "intelligence and experimental method is worth a trial" (LW 9:108) because we can be more sure that no other method will work.

It is consequently doubtful whether we should consider Dewey and Mead to be optimistic at all, even in the relative sense. Their approach to human action emphasizes, as John Herman Randall, Jr., notes, "the better, not the perfect."[27] It seems more sensible, then, to consider their approach to be not optimistic but melioristic. As Dewey writes, "Meliorism is the belief that the specific conditions which exist at one moment, be they comparatively bad or comparatively good, in any event may be bettered" (MW 12:181–82). Such a belief encourages intelligent action and arouses our confidence and hopefulness without dulling us into Emersonian passivity. A meliorism, in this sense, can underlie a philosophy of action that defends the possibility of change, reform, and progress through human effort. It is a faith that avoids the indolence of optimism and the paralysis of pessimism by placing its emphasis upon cooperative intelligence, upon action that is fallible yet guided by the best means we can employ.

As Dewey writes, "progress is not inevitable, it is up to men as individuals to bring it about. Change is going to occur anyway, and the problem is the control of change in a given direction" (LW 14:113). It is here that a philosophy of action—a social philosophy of social action—is so important. Dewey emphasizes that "a *mixture* of good and evil" exists, and "reconstruction in the direction of the good which is indicated by ideal ends, must take place, if at all, through continued cooperative effort" (LW 9:32). For Dewey and Mead, the possibility of improvement is rooted in their faith that others will rise to the call. It will consequently be necessary to look quite closely at this faith.

V

Dewey and Mead's view of the possibilities of human existence justifies courage and a belief in meliorism, which is undergirded by a faith. By this faith they mean a willingness to try, to take a chance; they both had faith that experience would continue to contain possibilities of solutions for human problems. Thinkers like them, Randall writes, "feel there is always more, the chance of new discoveries and fresh opportunities." No matter what has gone wrong, "we can always hope to *do* something about any situation."[28] From their standpoint, no situation is ever hopeless: "Any present always offers itself as a transition, a passage, or becoming," Dewey writes (LW 5:363). The situation thus contains emergent possibilities that, if properly cultivated, might be realized. Change for the better is in no way guaranteed, but it certainly is not impossible.

For Dewey, this kind of faith is a tendency toward action still rooted in "the dumb pluck of the animal" (MW 14:200). As William James recognized, it is a basic aspect of human life: "We cannot live or think at all without some degree of faith." It is this faith that enables us to act in spite of uncertainty. We live in a world without guarantees, in an evolving world where, as the Pragmatists recognized, the emergent aspects of situations—because they are emergent—cannot be fully anticipated. In this kind of world we need an experimental philosophy, one that guides us as we move onward. There are, as James recognizes, "cases where a fact cannot come at all unless a preliminary faith exists in its coming."[29] With regard to our social problems, this point is extremely important. As Dewey writes, because "we are part of the causes which bring them about in what we have done and have refrained from doing" (LW 9:131), we can influence their outcome by our actions. Our efforts are both definitely necessary and possibly efficacious.

The faith of Dewey and Mead in the possibilities of the future shows itself upon careful examination to be a cluster of faiths. There is first of all, in Dewey's words, a "faith in the capacities of human nature" (LW 11:219). On the same theme, Mead tells us that the individual "has a certain preciousness which cannot be estimated" (MT 411). Dewey adds that there are "uniquely distinctive qualities in each normal human being" (MW 13:297); given the proper means of self-development, "each individual has something to contribute" (LW 11:220). Thus their faith in individuals is also a faith in the possibilities of education as a means of freeing the minds of present and future political participants. This faith in individuals and "in the capacity of human beings for intelligent judgment and action if proper conditions are furnished" (LW 14:227) underlies democracy as the means to "the development of all the social capacities of every individual member of society" (MW 5:424). If we can develop individuals capable of intelligent social action, both Dewey and Mead feel we can legitimately have faith in our future possibilities.

The faith they rely on is admittedly unrelated to any guarantees of success. Yet it is still more than just a vague hope that these individuals will happen somehow upon adequate answers. Pragmatism's faith is a faith in the adequacy of our responses when we operate "in and through voluntary associations" (LW 3:144). Dewey and Mead have faith in democracy—"faith in our common human nature and in the power of voluntary action based upon public collective intelligence"—because they believe "in the power of pooled and cooperative experience" to solve our problems (LW 11:299, 219). This faith in democracy is thus related to their faith in science as a widely used method of problem solving; and, rejecting the distinction between the realms of nature and of history, this faith in democracy is bolstered by "what the method of experimental and cooperative intelligence has already accomplished in subduing to potential human use the energies of physical nature" (LW 11:64). The whole of this faith is reducible, Dewey writes, to "faith in the capacity of the intelligence of the common man to respond with commonsense to the free play of facts and ideas which are secured by effective guarantees of free inquiry, free assembly, and free communication" (LW 14:227). Dewey and Mead's belief that future problems will be solvable if approached in an intelligent and cooperative fashion by average people is thus the cornerstone of their social philosophy.

If we recognize that this faith is important to social life, we must commit ourselves to long-term endeavors to build democratic community: we must build, through our educational system, a wise citizenry that is both self-critical and concerned with social issues, and we must foster through our political institutions an involved citizenry that can both learn from and contribute to the common life. Through our crises we have learned, Dewey writes, that "every generation has to accomplish democracy over again for itself; that its very nature, its essence, is something that cannot be handed on from one person or one generation to another, but has to be worked out in terms of needs, problems and conditions of the social life of which, as the years go by, we are a part" (LW 13:299). Both Dewey and Mead believe that to have any hope of success as a society, we must develop democratic community. We need to abandon our attempts to short-circuit its slow and complex process of development through the quick fixes of technological breakthroughs or expert management, which lead only to new dependencies and new problems. The keynote of democracy for Dewey, as we have seen more than once already, is the necessity for "the participation of every mature human being" in the formation of the values that regulate our shared lives (LW 11:217). This kind of participatory democracy rooted in a well-developed community life is worthy, Dewey and Mead believe, of our faith.

VI

It is one matter to recognize the driving power that this faith in democracy has in the social thought of Dewey and Mead. It is yet another to attempt to evaluate it for our present situation. Many believe that it is unsatisfactory to ground a philosophy of social reform in faith and commitment. They want something more substantial, more tangible. Thus Thomas Vernor Smith writes sadly that, try as he might, he is unable "to discover in Mead's philosophy an adequate ground for his optimism regarding amelioration." Another writes that Dewey offers no more than a political faith that is "intended to be a substitute for religious faith" and that ultimately this approach means making "democracy itself dependent on faith."[30] Even if we remember that Dewey and Mead are not optimistic but melioristic, and even if we remember the difference between the kind of faith that they are advocating and its malignant Emersonian cousin,[31] there remains the need for some evaluation.

One evaluative approach would be to explore whether some set of circumstances might force Dewey and Mead to consider their faith in democracy a mistake. Is there, then, any conceivable situation in which they might be forced to conclude that their faith was misguided? The answer to this question is, of course, negative—no such set of circumstances exists. There are many possible sets of circumstances that might cause them to suggest a reconstruction of our political institutions or a reconstruction of our conceptions of key political terms like *democracy*. There are particular constellations of events that might cause some individuals, in Dewey's words, to "sag, withdraw and seek refuge" and even to "cave in" (MW 14:200) and abandon their personal faith in democracy. But there are no circumstances that would force Dewey and Mead to have to abandon democracy as having been repudiated. This assertion is part of what is meant by faith in democracy: a firm believer in democracy need recognize no set of facts as constituting its refutation. Next time things might turn out differently.

Critics, as might be expected, are greatly disturbed by the fact that no irresistible refutation is possible, and some, like Niebuhr, see this not as "faith" but rather as "blindness." As Georges Dicker writes, "the major reason why we do not abandon certain social plans which have not worked well in the past . . . is that we have ideals and values which we are unwilling to forego even if they are very hard to realize."[32] Mead admits exactly this. In our more-or-less successful struggle for the fully democratic ordering of society, he writes, "we are unwilling to surrender the ideal of such a government, if only for the sake of the exceptional occasions upon which it is realized, but more profoundly because we cherish the hope that the form of the institution in some ways helps toward the realization of what it promises" (SW 258). Thus, by keeping this ideal ever-present, we may be able to draw nearer to its realization.

Where the dispute arises is in Dicker's further point that, since the "scientific method recommends abandoning a hypothesis which is disconfirmed,"[33] we ought to abandon the democratic hypothesis and give up this faith. But has the hypothesis been disconfirmed? When blunders do occur, democrats like Dewey and Mead assume that they are not due to our permanent inability to act intelligently nor to human baseness—not due to a mistaken faith in democracy—but to poor educational systems, to trickery by politicians, to lag from prior situations, to mistaken estimates of the present context, and so on. In other words, past blunders are evidence for many conclusions—but not for the conclusion that faith in the possibilities of democracy is misguided.

True democrats do not hold themselves blameworthy for sticking with this faith in democracy. This faith does not mean, of course, that we should deny that mistakes have been made, for to do so would doom democracy. Neither does it mean that we may slough off future mistakes in a complacent anticipation of failure. What it does mean is that we must refuse to accede to the claim that broad-based self-government has been proven futile. Dewey writes: "The objection that the method of intelligence has been tried and failed is wholly aside from the point, since the crux of the present situation is that it has not been tried under such conditions as now exist. It has not been tried at any time with use of all the resources that scientific material and the experimental method now put at our disposal" (LW 11:37).[34] With modern educational possibilities and the growing technology of communication and with the greater integration of problems, information, and research, each new problematic situation is fundamentally new. As meliorists, believers in democracy must believe that we can improve upon prior efforts, that we do not know how far we can go until we have tried. It is only in this process of cooperative intelligence that the proper evaluation of the relevance of this melioristic faith for each occasion is possible.

VII

The prior discussion makes it clear that the question of the justifiability of faith in democracy has not been decided. Although Dewey and Mead are correct to reject claims of the disconfirmation of their hypothesis, they also recognize that it has not been confirmed either. Dewey, for example, admits that "there is no guarantee for optimism." However, he suggests that "there are resources within our grasp which, *if used,* will tend toward a favorable outcome" (LW 15:222). That is, this faith, however unproven in terms of past experience, may still be justifiable in terms of future experience; and, for Dewey and Mead, this faith is forward-looking. As Dewey writes, a philosophy should function as "a social hope reduced to a working program of action" (MW 11:43). In exactly this way "a philosophic faith, being a tendency to action, can be tried and tested only in action," and its realization, if it is to occur at all, "is in the future" (LW 5:278). The democratic ideal "expresses a postulate in the sense of a demand to be realized: That each individual shall have the opportunity for release, expression, fulfillment, of his distinctive capacities, and that the outcome shall further the establishment of a fund of shared values." Like other ideals, democracy "signifies something to be done" through the "constant meeting and solving of problems" rather than "something already given, something ready-made" (LW 7:350). Whatever evidence there may be remains to be created in the future, so present proof is impossible. It is possible, however, to examine the reasons Dewey and Mead offer for their acceptance of this faith: that democracy, if it is ever to work, requires faith and that, in the end, we really have no other choice.

Let us begin with the former claim: commitment to democratic action requires faith. If democracy is ever to work, Dewey writes, we must have faith because "in the long run democracy will stand or fall with the possibility of maintaining the faith [in the potentialities of human nature] and justifying it by works" (LW 13:152). For example, Mead writes that we may safely assume "the essentially social character of human impulse and endeavor," "the essentially social nature of their actions," and that human society is governed by relations of "solidarity" (SW 4). We may make these assumptions not because we have incontrovertible evidence that they are true, but because we believe that acting on them will help to make them come true. By our attitudes and our actions, Dewey and Mead believe, we can influence the degree to which, for example, solidarity does govern human relations. To attempt to bridge racial distrust or to rebuild local communities is to move beyond guarantees. As Dewey writes, "all endeavor for the better is moved by faith in what is possible, not by adherence to the actual" (LW 9:17). For both of them faith in democracy will increase the possibility of its success; pessimistic anticipation of failure will definitely contribute to failure. As long as our faith has some foundation, it is justified as well as it can be.

Second, although this faith may indicate to some, as we have seen, "an unrealistic over-confidence in man's unaided powers," to others—Dewey and Mead included—this criticism leads to the fundamental question of what other kinds of aid there might be. Dewey and Mead maintain that not only is it necessary that we have faith that democracy will work if we are ever to expect it to work, but also that there is no other method—not worship, prayer, following charismatic leaders, random actions, and so on—that is worthy of faith. The method of intelligence, tentative and hypothetical as it admittedly is, is all we have. "Reflective knowledge," Dewey asserts, is our "*only* means of regulation" (LW

4:175). And, unless we anticipate supernatural help, he continues, there is no sense in disparaging our attempts at intelligent reconstruction.[35] We have seen Mead's claim that, in problems of conduct, action is often required before we believe that we are ready. Dewey concurs: "The task is to go on, and not backward, until the method of intelligence and experimental control is the rule in social relations and social direction. Either we take this road or we admit that the problem of social organization in behalf of human liberty and the flowering of human capacities is insoluble" (LW 11:64). Thus, while progress is never inevitable, it is possible through conjoint effort "to bring it about" (LW 14:113).

This belief in the possibilities of democracy is thus not just a hope to be clutched but a faith to be worked with and built upon. Our democracy is, Dewey writes, "a fighting faith" (LW 11:64). To the extent that it makes sense to talk of "salvation" in our limited and uncaring world, "faith in the power of intelligence to imagine a future which is the projection of the desirable in the present, and to invent the instrumentalities of its realization, is our salvation" (MW 10:48). This melioristic sense of salvation, hypothetical and tentative, cooperative and active, is what Dewey and Mead offer us.

It may seem as though we are being forced to choose between two unattractive alternatives. On the one hand, we can risk being duped by committing ourselves to social efforts that have frequently failed; on the other, we can quit the common struggle and remain aloof spectators during others' attempts to advance the common good. Since I have been attacking the latter alternative throughout, it might seem that the former would be my choice; and it would, had I to make this choice. In this I agree with William James, who wrote that "worse things than being duped may happen to a man in this world."[36] This is not to deny that the costs of allowing ourselves to be duped are great. In our own present situation, where too often democracy has been reduced to governmental management of our acquiescence, where too often mistaken policies have been enthusiastically supported and attempted solutions fought, and—perhaps most significant for our theme of optimism— where too often electoral popularity can be correlated with the ability of public figures to make the voters feel good about themselves, the costs of being duped are very high. The way to react to these costs, however, is not to quietly accept them as a necessary concomitant of social commitment or, still less, to quit the common struggle. Rather, we should decrease the likelihood of our being duped by maintaining a self-conscious distance in our commitments.

One way to maintain this distance is never to allow this melioristic faith in cooperative intelligence to degenerate into jingoism. We must ever search ourselves to bring to light what Mead calls "the prejudices of the community" and work toward the fuller reality consistent with "the principles of the community" (MSS 217). We must even be ready, when necessary, "to fly in the face of the whole community" by appealing to the values of "a higher and better society than that which exists" (MSS 389).[37] A second restraint on this faith is that it cannot be allowed to become a delusion. Although we must have faith in the need for and in the efficacy of our actions, we cannot long succeed without a sense of humility, without a sense, as Dewey put it, "of our slight inability even with our best intelligence and effort to command events; a sense of our dependence upon forces that go their way without our wish and plan" (MW 14:200). In these two ways, and in others, we can develop a citizenry conscious of its own limitations and of the limitations on human action. And such a conscious citizenry, able to evaluate its own commitments, will go a long way toward breaking out of the unacceptable choice between quitting or being duped.

We have seen Carl Sandburg's admission that the people will be "tricked and sold and again sold." He tells us further that "the people is a lighted believer and hoper" and then wonders whether "this is to be held against them."[38] His answer is, of course, no. Dewey and Mead reply negatively as well. To believe and to hope, and to work to bring about the aims of our beliefs and hopes—all are necessary. Without such faith, social success is impossible because efforts at community building will not be undertaken. The Pragmatic social thinkers ask us to go out on a limb for the community, to commit ourselves to the welfare of the community beyond what seems justifiable under present experience. There are dangers to this commitment, as we have seen, but Dewey and Mead remain committed to the community because it is in and through the life of growing human community that we gain meaning and live well. Mead's formulation is brief: "All the things worth while are shared experiences" (MSS 385). Dewey's is more refined: "Within the flickering inconsequential acts of separate selves dwells a sense of the whole which claims and dignifies them. In its presence we put off mortality and live in the universal. The life of the community in which we live and have our being is the fit symbol of this relationship" (MW 14:227; cf. LW 1:157). Both of these formulations, and the body of Pragmatic social thought that stands behind each, indicate Dewey and Mead's belief in the importance of human community and their belief that with effort we can make the world a better place for all. The motive force behind these beliefs is not optimism. It is meliorism driven by faith.

8

Philosophers
and the Nature of Wisdom

Consider the following passage: "There are new things under the sun. Philosophers have a sense of social obligation today which they lacked only a short time ago. Not all of them, but most of them." These words, which sound as though they could have appeared in this week's *Chronicle of Higher Education,* in a current newsmagazine, or the latest issue of a contemporary philosophy journal, actually appeared in 1945. Their author, Max C. Otto, was writing at that time of what he saw as a shift in interest on the part of members of the philosophical community from "the advancement of philosophy as a profession" to the more general progress of society.[1] The timeliness of Otto's remarks for our own current situation, and their inappropriateness for most of the intervening period, point to the significant fact that the nature of philosophy and its place within the larger culture are in process. One of the factors in this change is the basic disagreement over whether the ultimate nature of the wisdom that we as philosophers are seeking is fundamentally intellectual or moral. This disagreement plays a role as well in our interpretation of the complex role of the philosopher in culture.

Philosophers carry out this cultural role in many ways. They attempt to grow through study and writing, and they generally teach as well, interpreting to future generations the ideas of the past. In a more limited way, philosophers also reproduce themselves through educating other philosophers. Philosophers, moreover, as residents of particular geographical areas and as citizens of various political units, have special social responsibilities to fulfill. The question I wish to consider here is whether these social responsibilities are part of the philosopher's responsibilities in a narrow philosophical sense or only in the broader human one. This question has been made more acute by professionalization.

"Professionalized philosophy" is a phrase we hear often these days. It encompasses various aspects of academic specialization and development: increasing separation into ever-smaller groups to focus upon ever-narrower topics with ever-sharper skills and ever-more-precise languages.[2] The professionalization of philosophy thus understood has made possible—or, better, has contributed to—many admitted advances for philosophy in our society. To point to just three, the professionalization of philosophy has led to a heightened social status for professors (at least in the eyes of administrators), has added security through systems of tenure and academic freedom, and has fueled the kind of technical improvements that are possible only with full-time consideration of limited topics. To point to these advances is, of course, not to deny the negative aspects of this professionalization: the denigration of undergraduate teaching as a valued and rewarded activity, the acceptance of centrifugal drift into clusters of specialists isolated from outsiders who cannot be expected to understand or appreciate what we are doing, and the loss of something to say to the broader community.

We—professionalized academics and our preprofessionalized students—too often forget that the higher education system in which we are participants does not belong to us. It was erected, at great social cost, by those who have gone before us. The quest for societal improvement, and the perceived role that intellectual inquiry was to play in this advance, are not just elements of a romantic fantasy on my part, as the briefest consideration of the history of almost all of our own institutions will show.[3] Our system of higher education, despite its many actual failings, has long been a major element in our society's concerted efforts to advance. It can thus, with some justification, be seen as a social institution with rights and privileges granted to it not on its own "natural" merits but only in relation to a set of duties. And it has frequently been seen to fail to perform these duties, as evidenced by William James's 1903 cry against the growing strangulation of the teaching mission of higher education by the Ph.D. "octopus,"[4] John Dewey's 1917 demand that philosophers forego "the problems of philosophers" and turn to "the problems of men" (MW 10:46), and the recommendations of the current stream of studies of academia in America.

II

The acceptance of isolated philosophers addressing the problems of philosophers is possible only within a society that accepts, in addition, isolated chemistry and literature professors and isolated geographers and poets. And, since the problem of isolated philosophers is really the problem of isolated intellectuals or scholars in general, perhaps a consideration of the broader intellectual terrain will help. One of the major contemporary American commentators on the problems of isolation and overspecialization is Wendell Berry. "The thing being made in a university is humanity," he writes of our ideal goal, although under our present fragmented situation, he admits, we are better described as "makers of *parts* of things." Of particular concern to Berry is the fact that we have allowed education to slip from being the means for creating "responsible heirs and members of human culture" to being a tool "to equip people to fulfill private ambitions." We have allowed this to happen because we have denied our own accountability for what our students do with their educational possibilities. He writes that, although "the responsibility to decide what to teach the young is an adult responsibility,"[5] we expect the young to decide for themselves what they ought to learn while operating under all of the limitations and pressures they must face as youths.

Academia's surrender of general education requirements was an especially harmful mistake, but it was one to be expected from those who, because of their isolation, recognize no responsibility. "The primary aspect of specialization is practical," Berry writes, and "the specialist withdraws from responsibility for everything not comprehended by his specialty."[6] Greater strides along narrower lines are, of course, possible for the specialist, and there is a certain rationality to having narrow tasks performed by those who understand them best; but, "from a public point of view, the specialist system is a failure because, though everything is done by an expert, very little is done well."[7] And higher education is a prime example of something not being done well, although certified experts perform almost all of its particular tasks.

A similar theme was sounded fifty years ago by Archibald MacLeish, who pilloried the intellectual class of his day for refusing to recognize and take up its social obligations. As MacLeish saw the situation, the paralysis of the intellectual class was due to "the division and therefore the destruction of intellectual responsibility." In earlier times this responsibility had been the hallmark of "the man of letters," but by MacLeish's day it was largely gone. "The single responsibility, the wholeness of function of the man of letters, has been replaced by the divided function, the mutual antagonism, the isolated irresponsibility of two figures, each free of obligation, each separated from a portion of his duty—the scholar and the writer." We have lost sight, MacLeish lamented, of the life of society as a continuous process ("the past made useful to the reasons of the present, the present understood against the knowledge of the past"), and the scholar who lives outside of the temporal process makes himself or herself "a refugee from consequences, an exile from the responsibilities of moral choice." The scholar, as we all know, "has his work to do. He has his book to finish." What once had been "a profession practiced for the common good," MacLeish saw as having become for the intellectuals of his day a "plump pigeon carcass to be picked at for his private pleasure and his private fame." In this new, irresponsible world, "scholarship may be more scientific," and "there are scholars of a scholarship as hard, as honest, as devoted as any we have known,"[8] but society in general is not thereby necessarily better off.[9]

It is possible to succeed at this narrow kind of scholarship without at the same time worrying about social advance only because such scholarship defines for itself what is to count as "success." We recognize, of course, that even if we operated in the light of a social criterion, most of what we do would probably turn out to have no important lasting social impact, and the impact of that portion of our work that did have an impact would be subject to numerous factors beyond our control. But this recognition is not a good reason for abandoning the social criterion itself and retreating to some specialist's criterion. As Merle E. Curti indicates, we need to recognize that "to avoid reference to the problems of the day and association with ordinary people, deprives intellectuals of valuable tests for their theories, as well as stimulating contact with American experience."[10] The recognition that the social criterion is not easily satisfied is similarly not a good reason for retreating to the comfortable criterion that any work that is likely to be publishable, or that research grant–giving agencies are likely to fund, is worth doing. Such irresponsible action cares not for the larger effects of the scholarly enterprise. And such isolation is possible only within the larger acceptance of intellectual isolation.

III

The isolation between intellectuals and the rest of society has not gone unnoticed, and it has generally been considered unfortunate. The proper response to this unfortunate situation, however, remains uncertain. In reply to the attacks on the isolation of professionalized philosophers has come an oft-repeated response from the ranks of those philosophers. This response concentrates, first, on the gap between the recognition of a problem, however severe, and the formulation of a solution to it and, second, on the methods by which solutions are formulated and advanced.

Beginning with the former, a frequently heard question is, How can *we* help? As individuals with specialized backgrounds in epistemology or in modal logic, in Spinoza's psychology or in Aristotle's metaphysics, what qualifications might we have for suggesting solutions to this or that social problem? Even granting, as many of these doubters will, that serious social problems exist, that we are citizens with obligations, and that we have intelligence, education, and leisure time, still they puzzle over what we can do. "By all means let us shed such light as we have on the problems of men," Arthur E. Murphy writes. "But if our light be darkness, how great is that darkness." We philosophers are very good at some kinds of inquiries, this response admits, but neither we as philosophers—nor linguists as linguists nor other types of professionalized intellectuals working as professionalized intellectuals—are likely to have anything particularly valuable to say about fundamental social problems.

The second aspect of the response to those who decry philosophers' lack of social involvement focuses on what often happens when narrowly trained experts do get involved in important social matters that are beyond their expertise (as almost all such matters are). Perhaps because they forget their lay status and allow themselves to hold excessively strong beliefs about what they do not know—about what no one can *know*—they often lose their normal good sense and stoop to what amounts to indoctrination. Engaged philosophers often give us pronouncements in place of thought, doctrines in place of inquiry. This is, however, as Murphy notes, "merely propaganda on axiological stilts." If the philosopher's "ruling passion is to serve mankind by *ad hoc* admonitions on urgent social issues, and if he is sure that he already knows *qua* philosopher how this salvation is to be achieved, then his governing concern will be to use philosophy as an instrument for the propagation of this saving doctrine and whatever does not fit this purpose will be condemned as incompetent, irrelevant and immaterial."[11] The net result of such attempts to benefit society will likely be negative.

The condemnation of the failure of isolated, professionalized philosophers to perform their legitimate social function thus meets with the dual response that these philosophers, as philosophers, can do little good and that frequently, by slipping from legitimate philosophizing, they do significant harm. The fundamental philosophical issue that underlies both aspects of the response here is the belief on the part of the critics that the wisdom that philosophers should be seeking is itself not something moral. This wisdom is, rather, intellectual. As May Brodbeck writes, it is better to conceive of philosophy "as contemplation" or "clarification and understanding" or "the search for answers to fundamental theoretical questions" rather than as "instrumental to action."[12] Philosophy is, in the words of Brand Blanshard, "an inquiry governed by a strictly intellectual end." In his view, "Philosophy as the attempt to understand the ultimate nature of things is an exacting and exhausting business which is almost certain to be badly done if the philosopher espouses the role of social reformer, and even worse done if he fails to see the difference between the roles." Blanshard, of course, recognizes the fact that the philosopher as a citizen should be concerned with the bettering of society, but involvement in reform activities "is not his business as a philosopher." In reality, "philosophy harnessed to a social program is not really philosophy at all, since it has surrendered its freedom of logical movement." All this follows, of course, if we assume that the wisdom that philosophy seeks is, as Blanshard suggests, intellectual in nature.[13] But should we make this assumption?

IV

No philosopher advocates short-sighted public action. Nor does any philosopher advocate the neglect of pressing social issues. We find, however, some philosopher-citizens whose deep conviction about, for example, the need to eliminate nuclear weapons has led them to write and speak and march in protest against them, and we find other philosopher-citizens whose conviction about these weapons is equally strong but leads them to act in favor of maintaining and upgrading them. Yet still other philosopher-citizens, although they are not necessarily uninformed about this issue or unmindful of its implications for the future well-being of society, do not get involved in the public debate.

I suggest that what divides the philosopher-citizens' practice between involvement and noninvolvement is the question of which philosophical sin they are more determined to avoid. Are they more wrong for getting involved in social actions that offer no guarantee of either correctness or success or for failing to get involved in efforts to address admittedly serious ills? Are they justified, because of the seriousness of the matter at hand, to take action in advance of complete certainty and to evaluate those who would hold back as overly cautious and hence morally wrong? Or does the seriousness of the issue justify their holding back from social action until more is known about the issues and the possible consequences of their social actions, so that they may view those who plunge ahead as reckless and hence morally wrong?

Philosophers like Murphy and Brodbeck and Blanshard tell us to hold back: the wisdom that we as philosophers seek is properly understood as intellectual in nature. Other philosophers, more closely aligned with Berry and MacLeish, answer differently. Among them are the Social Pragmatists. Consider, for example, the following position of Dewey: "The business of philosophy is intrinsically moral in its broadest human sense" (LW 16:366).[14] It is better for philosophy "to err in active participation in the living struggles and issues of its own age and times than to maintain an immune monastic impeccability, without relevancy and bearing in the generating ideas of its contemporary present." For him, philosophy pays its own way only by "sharing in the perplexities and failures, as well as in the joys and triumphs, of endeavor" (MW 4:142). In this approach, wisdom is fundamentally moral, not intellectual, in nature.

"By wisdom we mean not systematic and proved knowledge of fact and truth," Dewey writes, "but a conviction about moral values, a sense for the better kind of life to be led. Wisdom is a moral term. . . . it refers to a choice about something to be done, a preference for living this sort of life rather than that" (MW 11:44). The search for wisdom arises from the needs of people to overcome the problems of living. "To foresee consequences of existing conditions is to surrender neutrality and drift; it is to take sides in behalf of the consequences that are preferred" (LW 5:109–10). It is in this sense that Dewey could write that wisdom is "the application of what is known to intelligent conduct of the affairs of human life" (LW 15:157).

If the wisdom that we seek is a moral and practical pursuit, then philosophy has to become a social endeavor. Philosophy's social job is to help to create and sustain public dialogue about the problems and issues that the community is facing. Dewey writes that "contemporary society, the world over, is in need of more general and fundamental enlightenment and guidance than it now possesses" (MW 12:151). Since this help is not likely to just appear, we as philosopher-citizens must help to create it through advancing dialogue. Philosophy, Dewey writes, "can, if it has enduring courage and patience, engage cooperatively in the prolonged struggle to discover and utilize the positive ways and means by which the cause of human freedom and justice may be advanced in spite of the uncertainties, confusions, and active conflicts that now imperil civilization itself" (LW 16:418). This process of discovery not only omits the kind of propaganda that Murphy condemned, it positively precludes such propaganda. The change in our human condition that Dewey has in mind will be accomplished, he tells us, "only by the cooperative practical efforts of men of good will in all occupations and professions, not by philosophy itself" (LW 16:367). Only through cooperative inquiry, through debate and discussion, through the participation of all citizens in the formulation of social values, will our likelihood of success be advanced.

With this Pragmatic conception of public dialogue as our basis, we must foster the social role of the philosopher-citizens who choose to become socially active and to advocate involvement for others. We need to keep in mind, as we have seen above, that these individuals have no particular narrow expertise, as philosophers, for solving social problems. Philosopher-citizens who take stances for or against abortion or national policies with regard to Central America or animal rights do so—as did Dewey and the others when they advocated specific social stances—without any special *philosophical* knowledge. To recognize this is to yield little, however, because only by mistake do the philosopher-citizens whom we are considering root their philosophical warrant in such knowledge claims anyway. More properly, they see their philosophical warrant to be rooted, as did Dewey and Mead and Tufts before them, in the claim that wisdom is moral. What the activist philosopher-citizens are claiming to result from their philosophical insight, then, is a heightened sense of commitment to the process of addressing social issues through cooperative inquiry. This clearly is a moral rather than an intellectual claim.

V

It is here that we can see the fundamental difference between the spirit of the Social Pragmatists and that of neo-Pragmatists like Richard Rorty. His work demonstrates, of course, fundamental and significant continuities with the earlier writers. For example, in good Social Pragmatist fashion Rorty has justly attacked philosophy's arrogant and bullying claims to intellectual primacy, its self-appointed role of "keeping the other disciplines honest."[15] And he has demonstrated the need for philosophy to remake itself so that it can return from its "withdrawal from the rest of the academy and from culture," which was undertaken in defense of its own "autonomy,"[16] to take up again a contributory role in the broader life of humankind. For too long, Rorty maintains, philosophy has seen its role as preparatory and negative rather than ongoing and contributory. For too long philosophy has mistaken its pursuit of cleverness for the pursuit of wisdom.[17] In this he agrees with Dewey, who writes that philosophy must abandon its tendency toward "refining and polishing tools to be used . . . only in refining more tools of precisely the same kind" (LW 16:411). When we ask what these tools more properly should be used for, however—when we ask what philosophy will contribute on its return—the clear differences between Rorty and the Social Pragmatists emerge.

The goal that Rorty has in mind for this reconstructed philosophy is "keeping a conversation going."[18] By this he means, negatively, that we must prevent philosophy from adopting the kind of supremacist pretensions that he has just rejected. Positively, "keeping a conversation going" means engaging in a cooperative and interdisciplinary intellectual activity of clarification and description, "an activity which is its *own* end."[19] Our philosophical goal here is to "edify," by which Rorty means to help "readers, or society as a whole, break free from outworn vocabularies and attitudes" rather than to attempt "to provide 'grounding' for the institutions and customs of the present."[20] Whatever value is to be found in Rorty's conception of the philosophic endeavor—and I believe that it is considerable, especially when contrasted with the conception of philosophy as self-appointed intellectual referee—its difference from the Social Pragmatists' is clear. From even this brief glance we can see that the Pragmatism that Rorty is advocating is built around an intellectual sense of wisdom, not the moral sense of wisdom found in Pragmatic social thought.

The intellectual conception of wisdom that informs Rorty's Pragmatism, combined with his explicit desire to have philosophy adopt a spirit of "playfulness" and a more "relaxed attitude,"[21] would leave this reconstructed philosophy without teeth, unable to perform its necessary critical task of helping us, in Dewey's words, "to discriminate between ends that merely seem good and those which are really so—between specious, deceptive goods, and lasting true goods" (LW 7:181). Thus Rorty's Pragmatism loses the central emphasis of Social Pragmatists: the importance of ongoing critical inquiry to attempt to make living more worthwhile. "Our future," John J. McDermott writes in the latter spirit, "does not await some natural or divine *deus ex machina*." Rather, it "hangs in the balance, awaiting the outcome of our deliberate, willing, and intelligent efforts to remediate, to heal, and to blunt and shunt those destructive forces which seem inevitably to accompany our journey."[22] Increasingly as we move into our ever-more-interdependent future, we will have to reconstruct our values and our institutions. To do this successfully we will need to work together as a community of critical inquirers, evaluating our options and their potential consequences. And we will need to maintain our "spirit of seriousness," in spite of Rorty's recommendations to the contrary.[23]

It is the position of the Social Pragmatists that philosophical inquiry has a vital, participatory role to play in this social process. It is, moreover, a role that reconnects philosophy with a responsible role in education because, Dewey writes, "education is the most far-reaching and most fundamental way of correcting social evils and meeting social issues" (LW 5:297). Rorty's Pragmatism offers no connection between philosophy and education, and his intellectual understanding of wisdom rejects involvement in social inquiry. Perhaps he takes this position because he fears that philosophy will slip back into bullying or that there is no "market" for such involvement[24] or that philosophy simply cannot help. But the task of social reconstruction still remains to be done somehow. Philosophy, used in the way that the Social Pragmatists have developed, should be able to help—if we are willing to undertake the task.

VI

Living the life of philosophy impels the search for wisdom. The question of the degree of social involvement that is proper to this philosophical life will not be settled, however, until the term *wisdom* itself is finally defined; since defining it is fundamentally stipulative, a settlement seems unlikely. Whatever *our* definition of philosophy is to be, *we* will bear the responsibility for having chosen it. Some philosophers will continue to seek wisdom of the intellectual sort, others of the moral. Calls will continue for increased involvement in social questions on the part of philosophers, as well as condemnations of unjustified stances; suggestions that intellectuals avoid still-murky practical issues will go on, as well as condemnations of the intellectual shirking of responsibility. My sympathies, based in the Social Pragmatist criterion of attempting to advance the common good, are with Berry and MacLeish, with Dewey and Mead and Tufts. Intellectuals have responsibilities beyond the furtherance of their disciplines. If wisdom is a moral goal, as I believe it is, then we, the favored, must address social ills. As Max C. Otto wrote in 1945, the struggle to release humans "from thoughtless action and narrowness of spirit, and to aid them toward wisdom of life and broad good will, has been the philosopher's battle from the beginning, and it is his battle in a peculiar and crucial sense today."[25] From the perspective of the Social Pragmatists, it is a battle without guarantees and a battle without end. But is it not a battle without reward.

In 1922 in the wake of the horror of the First World War, Dewey wrote that we could still recover our sense of our social whole. "Infinite relationships of man with his fellows and with nature already exist," he writes. "Even in the midst of conflict, struggle and defeat a consciousness is possible of the enduring and comprehending whole" (MW

14:226). This fact remains unchanged to this day, and it seems unlikely to change in the foreseeable future. Our conflicts and struggles, our victories and defeats, can knit us together, or they can tear us apart. Pragmatic social thought emphasizes the possibility of the former, and it calls us to actions to attempt to actualize this community.

Much remains to be done in recovering Pragmatic social thought. This volume is only a very small piece of a very large task. Other contributors remain to be considered; other topics, to be included and explored. Connections with alternative views need to be delineated, and criticisms need to be updated and reevaluated. But, most important, the recovery of Pragmatic social thought, if it remains only an intellectual recovery, will be of little value. If it does not become an inspirational and practical tool in efforts to carry on the actual reconstruction of democratic community, this recovery will serve no social purpose. Social Pragmatism will be just another trinket in a culture conceived of as "an adornment of life rather than an interpretation of life," as Mead put it, just another slice of decorative culture "in [the] form of cake, not in the form of daily bread."[26]

The driving spirit of Pragmatic social thought can be encapsulated in the following comment by Tufts: "No individual counts much through his own resources."[27] In spite of the central moral importance that individuals have, as the focus of our existence, they live their lives amid communities and institutions—traditions, values, practices, and goals—that need to undergo ongoing evaluation and, on occasion, modification. To build a better world for individuals now and in the future it is necessary for us to have ongoing cooperative efforts to carry out these evaluations and modifications. It is in this way that the community reconstructs.

NOTES

Chapter 1. Introduction: Pragmatic Social Thought

1. I have discussed the problem of presenting a picture of Pragmatism without a consideration of its social thought elsewhere. See my "Rorty's Use of Dewey," and "Ayer and Pragmatism."

2. See Joseph L. Blau, *Men and Movements in American Philosophy;* Herbert W. Schneider, *A History of American Philosophy;* Elizabeth Flower and Murray G. Murphey, *A History of Philosophy in America;* H. S. Thayer, *Meaning and Action: A Critical History of Pragmatism.*

3. See Philip P. Wiener, *Evolution and the Founders of Pragmatism;* Edward H. Madden, *Chauncey Wright and the Foundations of Pragmatism;* Madden, *Chauncey Wright;* Max H. Fisch, *Peirce, Semeiotic, and Pragmatism.*

4. In this volume I will be quoting passages from Peirce's writings from *The Collected Papers of Charles Sanders Peirce,* ed. Charles Hartshorne, Paul Weiss, and Arthur W. Burks.

5. Ibid., 1.7; cf. 5.265, 7.54.

6. Ibid., 5.407; cf. 5.565–73.

7. Ibid., 1.135.

8. See ibid., 1.13, 5.358; Justus Buchler, *Charles Peirce's Empiricism,* 74–78.

9. Peirce, *Collected Papers,* 5.467, 5.464, 5.403–10.

10. Ibid., 5.412.

11. In this volume I will be quoting passages from William James's writings where possible from the Critical Edition of *The Works of William James,* edited by Frederick H. Burkhardt et al. The individual works are listed in the Bibliography.

12. James, *Pragmatism: A New Name for Some Old Ways of Thinking,* 28; cf. his *Essays in Philosophy,* 124–28.

13. I am rejecting here the view of Ralph Barton Perry: "Perhaps it would be correct, and just to all parties, to say that the modern movement known as pragmatism is largely the result of James's misunderstanding of Peirce" (*The Thought and Character of William James,* ed. Perry, 2:409).

14. James, *Essays in Philosophy,* 124; cf. *Pragmatism,* 28–30.

15. *Essays in Philosophy*, 129, 131; cf. James, *The Meaning of Truth: A Sequel to Pragmatism*, 5–6.

16. *Pragmatism*, 34; cf. ibid., 96–97; *The Meaning of Truth*, 3–10.

17. *Pragmatism*, 40.

18. See Thayer, *Meaning and Action*, 146–59, 527–56; Ellen Kappy Suckiel, *The Pragmatic Philosophy of William James;* and my "Ayer and Pragmatism."

19. James, *Pragmatism*, 36.

20. Peirce, *Collected Papers*, 5.375.

21. In this volume I will be quoting passages from John Dewey's writings from the Critical Edition of his works edited by Jo Ann Boydston, abbreviated as follows:

EW *The Early Works of John Dewey, 1882–98*
MW *The Middle Works of John Dewey, 1899–1924*
LW *The Later Works of John Dewey, 1925–53*

22. See Dewey, LW 12:15–16; LW 14:168–88; Thayer, *Meaning and Action*, 193–94; Ralph W. Sleeper, *The Necessity of Pragmatism: John Dewey's Conception of Philosophy*, 134–67.

23. In this volume I will be quoting passages from George Herbert Mead's works, when possible, from the University of Chicago series, abbreviated as follows:

MSS *Mind, Self, and Society from the Standpoint of a Social Behaviorist*
MT *Movements of Thought in the Nineteenth Century*
PA *The Philosophy of the Act*
PP *The Philosophy of the Present*
SW *Selected Writings*

24. I have examined Tufts's life and thought in my introduction to *Selected Writings of James Hayden Tufts*.

25. Tufts, "The Institution as Agency of Stability and Readjustment in Ethics," 139–40.

26. Tufts, "The University and the Advance of Justice," 192.

Chapter 2. William James and the Ethics of Fulfillment

1. Josiah Royce, *William James and Other Essays on the Philosophy of Life*, 31. Cf. Perry, *The Thought and Character of William James*, 2:250; John Wild, *The Radical Empiricism of William James*, 259; Thayer, *Meaning and Action*, 147; Abraham Edel, "Notes on the Search for a Moral Philosophy in William James," 245; Dewey, MW 6:92; LW 2:14; LW 14:101.

2. Quoted in Perry, *The Thought and Character of William James*, 2:264; cf. James, *The Will to Believe and Other Essays in Popular Philosophy*, 146.

3. James, *The Will to Believe*, 150.

4. *The Letters of William James*, 1:148; *The Will to Believe*, 141.

5. *Pragmatism*, 115; cf. *The Will to Believe*, 152.

6. *Pragmatism*, 125; *The Will to Believe*, 141.

7. James, *The Principles of Psychology*, 277; cf. John J. McDermott, "A Metaphysics of Relations: James' Anticipation of Contemporary Experience," esp. 86–90.

8. James, *Talks to Teachers*, 134.

9. Julien Benda, "The Attack on Western Morality," 416. A necessary antidote to this article is Dewey's "William James' Morals and Julien Benda's" (LW 15:19–26).

10. James, *The Will to Believe*, 154; *Talks to Teachers*, 132, 138.

11. *Talks to Teachers*, 166.

12. Ibid., 149, 151, 149; cf. *The Will to Believe*, 154–55.

13. *Pragmatism*, 142; *The Will to Believe*, 27.

14. *The Will to Believe*, 153, 158.

15. Perry, *The Thought and Character of William James*, 2:264; cf. Sidney Hook, *Pragmatism and the Tragic Sense of Life*, 13.

16. Max C. Otto, "On a Certain Blindness in William James," 187, 188, 185.

17. The term "advantages" is, of course, Santayana's. Cf. his *Character and Opinion in the United States*, 64. On the point of advantages, Otto compares James unfavorably with his sister, Alice. Alice, though a co-sharer in the advantages and though willing to remain what she called "a bloated capitalist," could still admire the beauty of the solidarity of the workers and abhor the savagery of the ruling class (Otto, "On a Certain Blindness," 184–85). Alice James writes further of the moral superiority of the workers to those in power, "who have every opportunity for acquiring wisdom, inheriting noble, humane and generous instincts [yet] have found no more inspired means of allaying their mutual rapacities than shooting down vast hordes of innocent men, as helpless as sheep " (*The Diary of Alice James*, 113).

18. Otto, "On a Certain Blindness," 189.

19. Vivian J. McGill, "Pragmatism Reconsidered: An Aspect of John Dewey's Philosophy," 291; cf. Otto, "On a Certain Blindness," 190.

20. George R. Garrison and Edward H. Madden, "William James—Warts and All," 207, 211; cf. C. Wright Mills, *Sociology and Pragmatism: The Higher Learning in America*, 260–68, 273–74.

21. Cf. James, *Essays in Religion and Morality*, 171–73; *Talks to Teachers*, 155; *The Principles of Psychology*, 129.

22. *Talks to Teachers*, 166; cf. *Essays in Religion and Morality*, 170. The thoroughness of James's rejection of revolutionary alternatives is perhaps most clearly indicated by his casual remarks, like his statement that it is only habit that "saves the children of fortune from the envious uprisings of the poor" (*The Principles of Psychology*, 125).

23. *Talks to Teachers*, 162, 161.

24. Otto, "On a Certain Blindness," 189. Otto is quoting from *The Letters of William James*, 2:90; cf. 2:101.

25. Arthur E. Murphy, "Philosophical Scholarship," 180.

26. Otto, "On a Certain Blindness," 190. There is, of course, more than a little truth to this. Those of us who are quick to point out James's failure to

recognize "obvious" problems in his day must be prepared to be tried ourselves
for values we now fail to recognize and evils against which we fail to take action.

27. Merle E. Curti, *The Social Ideas of American Educators*, 458.

28. John E. Smith, *The Spirit of American Philosophy*, 78.

29. James, *Pragmatism*, 55; *The Will to Believe*, 134.

30. *Pragmatism*, 55; *The Varieties of Religious Experience*, 406.

31. Mead, for example, believed that human society was "not only as much
as but more at home on the earth than any other species of life that has existed
here" (PA 508).

32. James, *Talks to Teachers*, 150.

33. *The Will to Believe*, 157.

34. *Essays in Religion and Morality*, 165.

35. Ibid., 162, 168, 170, 165.

36. Ibid., 162, 164, 171, 172.

37. See Curti, *The Social Ideas of American Educators*, 432–33; Mead, "National-Mindedness and International-Mindedness," 385–407.

38. Dewey continued that pessimism is not justified because "continual
search and experimentation to discover the meaning of changing activity, keeps
activity alive, growing in significance" (MW 14:144–45).

39. James, *Pragmatism*, 43. The list of others who sought such "moral holidays" would include Morris R. Cohen, Irwin Edman, and Reinhold Niebuhr.
Cf. Cohen, *A Preface to Logic*, 202; Cohen, *American Thought: A Critical Sketch*,
296–97; Edman, *Philosopher's Holiday*, 268; and Niebuhr, *Leaves from the Notebook
of a Tamed Cynic*, 112–13.

40. Cited by James in *Essays in Religion and Morality*, 110; cf. *Journals and
Miscellaneous Notebooks of Ralph Waldo Emerson*, 13:80.

Chapter 3. George Herbert Mead on Intelligent Social Reconstruction

1. Walter Lippmann, *Drift and Mastery: An Attempt to Diagnose the Current
Unrest*, 266.

2. H. L. Mencken, *Notes on Democracy*, 202, 211.

3. Edward Lee Thorndike, "The Psychology of the Half-Educated Man,"
670.

4. William Zebulon Foster, *Toward Soviet America*, 255, 276, 213.

5. Emerson, "Ode," in *The Complete Works of Ralph Waldo Emerson*, 9:78.

6. Joseph Wood Krutch, *The Measure of Man*, 25, 17.

7. Mead fares much better in such studies as Darnell Rucker, *The Chicago
Pragmatists;* David L. Miller, *George Herbert Mead: Self, Language and the World;*
S. Morris Eames, *Pragmatic Naturalism: An Introduction;* and Thayer, *Meaning
and Action*.

8. For a fuller presentation of the theme of reconstruction in Mead's thought
than is presented here, see my "George Herbert Mead: Philosophy and the
Pragmatic Self," 91–114.

9. Mead, "The Philosophy of John Dewey," 75.

10. Kenneth Burke, "George Herbert Mead," 292.

11. Peirce, *Collected Papers*, 5.358–87; James, *The Will to Believe*, 57.

12. Mead, review of Gustave Le Bon, *The Psychology of Socialism*, 406.

13. James, *The Will to Believe*, 79.

14. Mead, review of Jane Addams, *The Newer Ideals of Peace*, 124.

15. Mead, "The Social Settlement: Its Basis and Function," 110.

16. Thorstein Veblen, *The Theory of the Leisure Class*, 224.

17. Herbert Hoover, *The Challenge to Liberty*, 60–61.

18. See Jane Addams's attempt to understand and describe the complex relationship between the party boss and the local citizenry in Mead's own Chicago—a relationship in which the residents see the boss as "a true Robin Hood" and as an individual who, as she suggests one such resident might put it, "knows the poor better than the big guns who are always about talking civil service and reform" ("Ethical Survivals in Municipal Corruption," 285, 282).

19. Mead, *The Conscientious Objector*, second page.

20. Paul E. Pfuetze, *Self, Society, Existence: Human Nature and Dialogue in the Thought of George Herbert Mead and Martin Buber*, 239.

21. Mead, review of Thorstein Veblen, *The Nature of Peace and the Terms of Its Perpetuation*, 762.

22. Niebuhr, *Moral Man and Immoral Society: A Study in Ethics and Politics*, 3, 44.

23. Thomas Vernor Smith, "The Social Philosophy of George Herbert Mead," 381, 383.

24. See Perry, *Puritanism and Democracy*, 381.

25. Pfuetze, *Self, Society, Existence*, 238.

26. Mead, "Bishop Berkeley and His Message," 430.

Chapter 4. John Dewey's Method of Social Reconstruction

1. Franklin Delano Roosevelt, *The Public Papers and Addresses of Franklin Delano Roosevelt*, 1:646, 659.

2. Clarke A. Chambers, *Seedtime of Reform: American Social Service and Social Action, 1918–33*, 249.

3. Arthur M. Schlesinger, Jr., "Reinhold Niebuhr's Role in American Political Thought and Life," 140–41.

4. See Alan P. Grimes, *American Political Thought*, 418–42; George H. Sabine, "The Pragmatic Approach to Politics," 865–85.

5. Charles Frankel, "John Dewey's Legacy," 317–18. Frankel's view that it is difficult to determine where Dewey stood is complicated by his own admission that Dewey "was not afraid to take sides in public controversies" (317) and by his later claim that Dewey's "views on concrete social, political, and educational issues were equivocal, often changeable, and . . . never summarizable in a neat form" ("John Dewey's Social Philosophy," 8).

6. Thayer, *Meaning and Action*, 446.

7. Morton White, *Science and Sentiment in America*, 289; cf. White, *Social Thought in America: The Revolt Against Formalism*, 201.

8. There are many other such critics. Sidney Kaplan writes, for example, that "despite [Dewey's] ceaseless plea to others to deal realistically with public problems, the fatal flaw of his own thought has been precisely the absence of a usable politics" ("Social Engineers as Saviors: Effects of WWI on Some American Liberals," 348). In his notes to this piece, Kaplan refers to at least half a dozen other like-minded critics.

9. See Dewey, MW 11:122–26, 388–92; MW 15:53–64, 87–127, 383–417; LW 8:13–18. Cf. also Joseph Ratner's discussion of the Outlawry movement, *Intelligence in the Modern World: John Dewey's Philosophy*, 525–66.

10. See, e.g., George E. Axtelle and Joe R. Burnett, "Dewey on Education and Schooling," 257–305.

11. See George Dykhuizen, *The Life and Mind of John Dewey*; Edward J. Bordeau, "Dewey's Ideas about the Great Depression," 67–84; Richard J. Brown, "John Dewey and the League for Independent Political Action," 156–61.

12. See Dewey, LW 9:249–90, 296–98.

13. Dewey's position here thus avoids Brand Blanshard's criticism of socially involved philosophies: "If each [philosopher] were to give himself to social reform, claiming for his particular program the sanction of philosophy, that discipline would be rapidly drained of both meaning and public regard" ("Can the Philosopher Influence Social Change?" 750). I will return to this theme in chapter 8.

14. Buchler, *The Concept of Method*, 145. For studies of Dewey's understanding of method, see ibid., 145–54; Cohen, "Some Difficulties in Dewey's Anthropocentric Naturalism," 196–228; James E. McClellan, "Dewey and the Concept of Method: Quest for the Philosopher's Stone in Education," 213–28; Joseph G. Metz, "Democracy and the Scientific Method in the Philosophy of John Dewey," 242–62.

15. The volumes are, in order, *Democracy and Education* (MW 9), *The Public and Its Problems* (LW 2), *Experience and Nature* (LW 1), *The Quest for Certainty* (LW 4), and *How We Think* (LW 8).

16. Dewey writes: "Probably there is in the consciously articulated ideas of every thinker an over-weighting of just those things that are contrary to his natural tendencies, an emphasis upon those things that are contrary to his intrinsic bent, and which, therefore, he has to struggle to bring to expression, while the native bent, on the other hand, can take care of itself" (LW 5:150).

17. Cf. Clarence E. Ayres's misguided criticism that Dewey fails to offer such a system in "Philosophy and Genius," 263–71.

18. See, e.g., Dewey, MW 2: 306–7; LW 8:199–209; LW 12:105–22.

19. This particular point has been a stumbling block to many readers. Cf. the following critics, who point to the essential importance of the user of the method as a *criticism* of Dewey: Burke, "Liberalism's Family Tree," 115; Edwin

A. Burtt, "The Core of Dewey's Way of Thinking," 418; Richard Hofstadter, *Anti-intellectualism in American Life,* 372–77.

20. See Dewey, LW 1:325–26; LW 4:211–12, 217; LW 13:273.

21. See Peirce's similar sense in his discussion of the various "methods" for settling doubt in his *Collected Papers,* 5.358–87.

22. The term *level* is my own, and I use it to describe the two distinguishable stages within the ongoing process of social reconstruction. I prefer this term to others, like *phase* or *aspect,* in spite of its adverse spatial connotations, because I think that it best captures Dewey's sense of experience *penetrating* into nature, "reaching down into its depths," tunneling "in all directions," and bringing "to the surface things at first hidden." (LW 1:11). In just this way, intellectual reconstruction uncovers and brings to the surface of public discussion the facts, ideas, and suggestions that play such an important role in the level of institutional reconstruction.

23. See, e.g., William H. Brickman, "Dewey's Social and Political Commentary," 218–56.

24. May Brodbeck, "Philosophy in America, 1900–1950," in *American Non-Fiction,* ed. Brodbeck et al., 44.

25. Albert W. Levi, *Philosophy and the Modern World,* 323.

26. Wilmon H. Sheldon, "Professor Dewey, the Protagonist of Democracy," 312.

27. Lippmann, *The Public Philosophy,* 27–28.

28. Thorndike, "The Psychology of the Half-Educated Man," 670.

29. Frankel, "John Dewey's Social Philosophy," 18–19.

30. See, e.g., Wendell Berry's discussion of technology on the farm in "Living in the Future: The 'Modern' Agricultural Ideal," in *The Unsettling of America: Culture and Agriculture,* 51–79.

31. See the revisionist critique of the nature and influence of Dewey's philosophy of education contained in the following representative pieces: Walter Feinberg, "The Conflict between Intelligence and Community in Dewey's Educational Philosophy," 236–48; Clarence Karier, "Making the World Safe for Democracy: A Historical Critique of John Dewey's Pragmatic Liberal Philosophy in the Warfare State," 12–47; and N. C. Bhattacharya, "Demythologizing John Dewey," 117–23.

32. C. Wright Mills, *The Power Elite,* 317.

33. Cf. Abraham Lincoln's statement that "no man is good enough to govern another man, *without that other's consent*" (reply to Senator Douglas at Peoria, Illinois, October 16, 1854, in *The Collected Works of Abraham Lincoln,* 2:266).

34. James Gouinlock, "Philosophy and Moral Values: The Pragmatic Analysis," 103.

35. Tufts and Dewey, *Ethics* (MW 5:443–44).

36. Cf. the similarity of this position to James's view: "*The treating of a name as excluding from the fact named what the name's definition fails positively to include, is what I call 'vicious intellectualism'* " (*A Pluralistic Universe,* 32).

37. Mills, *Sociology and Pragmatism,* 405.

Chapter 5. Politics and Conceptual Reconstruction

1. One excellent source that discusses aspects of this understanding of human nature is Russell Kirk, *The Conservative Mind: From Burke to Eliot.*

2. See, e.g., Abraham Lincoln's classic formulation of the view that we must defend the "correct" meanings of terms in his example of the sheep and the wolf who "are not agreed upon a definition of the word liberty," and in his consequent advocacy of the need to repudiate "the wolf's dictionary" (Address at the Sanitary Fair in Baltimore, April 18, 1864, *Collected Works,* 7:302).

3. Oliver Wendell Holmes, Jr., *Towne v. Eisner,* 245 U.S. 425 (1917).

4. Lippman, *A Preface to Politics,* 169.

5. James, *The Varieties of Religious Experience,* 30, 32; James, *A Pluralistic Universe,* 36; cf. 32.

6. Charles Horton Cooley, *Human Nature and the Social Order,* 395; *Social Organization,* 379; *Human Nature and the Social Order,* 395.

7. Tufts, "The Community and Economic Groups," 597.

8. Some interesting aspects of the history of the idea of democracy in America are explored in Charles A. Beard and Mary R. Beard, *America in Midpassage,* 920–49; Charles A. Beard, *The Republic: Conversations on Fundamentals,* 27–37; and Curti, *Probing Our Past,* 3–31.

9. White, *Social Thought in America,* 165. White is here criticizing Dewey's reconstruction of the terms *force* and *violence* in his analysis of pacifism in World War I. Cf. Dewey, MW 10:211–15, 244–51, 276–80.

10. Thomas Vernor Smith, *The Philosophic Way of Life,* 10–11.

11. Santayana, *Character and Opinion in the United States,* 148.

12. Peirce, *Collected Papers,* 5.13. The full passage reads as follows: "If philosophy is ever to stand in the ranks of the sciences, literary elegance must be sacrificed—like the soldier's old brilliant uniforms—to the stern requirements of efficiency, and the philosophist must be encouraged—yea, and required—to coin new terms to express such new scientific concepts as he may discover, just as his chemical and biological brethren are expected to do."

13. Cf. Dewey, LW 16:387–89; LW 1:361–64; Corliss Lamont, "New Light on Dewey's *Common Faith,*" 22–25.

14. Similar views can be found in the works of such writers as William Ernest Hocking, who writes that we ought to look for the *"fighting-value"* of political discourse. "I owe much to the habit, painfully acquired, of looking for the meaning of terms and propositions in what they lead to, and especially in what they lead us to do" ("Action and Certainty," 19–20). Another figure who saw political discourse in similar terms was Vernon Louis Parrington, who writes that ideas "are weapons hammered out on the anvil of human needs. . . . To consider the sword apart from the struggle is to turn dilettante and a frequenter of museums" (quoted in Vernon Louis Parrington, Jr., "Vernon Parrington's View: Economics and Criticism," 99). See also Curti's *Human Nature in American Thought: A History* for a historical survey of understandings of human nature with a clear recognition of the rhetorical power of the term *human nature.*

Chapter 6. Freedom and Community

1. John Locke, *The Second Treatise of Government*, paragraphs 124, 123.

2. Friedrich A. Hayek, *The Road to Serfdom*, 15.

3. Adam Smith, *Lectures on Jurisprudence*, 347; *An Inquiry into the Nature and Causes of the Wealth of Nations*, 25.

4. Smith, *The Wealth of Nations*, 285; cf. 454.

5. Smith, *Lectures on Jurisprudence*, 489; cf. *The Wealth of Nations*, 22.

6. Although he does not emphasize the problems with the division of labor, Smith is cognizant of the fact that this national wealth comes at great cost to the individual workers. Cf., for example, *Lectures on Jurisprudence*, 539–40; *The Wealth of Nations*, 781–82.

7. Smith, *The Wealth of Nations*, 454. Smith also offers often-overlooked, weaker versions of the actions of the "invisible hand": the individual "intends only his own gain, and he is in this, as in *many* other cases, led by an invisible hand to promote an end which was no part of his intention. *Nor is it always the worse* for the society that it was no part of it. By pursuing his own interest he *frequently* promotes that of the society more effectually than when he really intends to promote it" (ibid., 456, emphasis added). Cf. ibid., 454; Smith, *The Theory of Moral Sentiments*, 184–85.

8. Carl Becker, "New Liberties for Old," 112.

9. Tufts, "The Institution as Agency of Stability and Readjustment in Ethics," 145–46.

10. Tufts, "A Social Philosopher's Idea of Good Government," 195; cf. Tufts, "The Institution as Agency of Stability and Readjustment in Ethics," 145.

11. William Graham Sumner,"The Challenge of Facts," in *The Challenge of Facts and Other Essays*, 25.

12. Sumner, "The Forgotten Man," in *The Forgotten Man and Other Essays*, 476, 466, 493, 473.

13. From this point of view, the peregrinations of many from New Left to Wall Street seem more easily understandable.

14. Henry David Thoreau, *Walden*, 8, 90, 326.

15. Ibid., 91, 90, 33.

16. Thoreau, *Reform Papers*, 70, 64, 65, 136.

17. Ibid., 74, 84, 71, 73–74.

18. Herbert Hoover, *The Challenge to Liberty*, 1–2; cf. 194–95; Hoover, *American Individualism*, 21–22; Robert Nozick, *Anarchy, State, and Utopia*, 50.

19. David E. Lilienthal, *TVA: Democracy on the March*, 75.

20. Hayek, *The Constitution of Liberty*, 17.

21. Wendell Berry, *The Gift of Good Land*, 112; Berry, *A Continuous Harmony*, 156, 66, 67.

22. Berry, *The Hidden Wound*, 118.

23. Robert N. Bellah et al., *Habits of the Heart: Individualism and Commitment in American Life*, 282, 163.

24. Fred Hirsch, *Social Limits of Growth*, 27, 5, 52, 9; cf. 37, 67, 168.

25. Roosevelt, *Public Papers and Addresses*, 11:53–54.

26. Hayek, *The Road to Serfdom*, 158; cf. Hayek, *The Constitution of Liberty*, 16–17.

27. Becker, "New Liberties for Old," 102.

28. Hayek, *The Road to Serfdom*, 157, 159; cf. Hayek, *The Constitution of Liberty*, 16–17.

29. Tufts, "The Present Significance of Scholarship," 6.

30. Cf. Hayek, *The Constitution of Liberty*, 421 n.1.

31. Hayek, *The Road to Serfdom*, 25–26.

32. Ibid., 25, 106, 79; cf. Hayek, *The Constitution of Liberty*, 11–13, 20–21, 85–88.

33. Tufts, "The Community and Economic Groups," 597.

34. Hoover, *American Individualism*, 48.

35. Hayek, *The Road to Serfdom*, 25.

36. Peter T. Manicas, *The Death of the State*, 244.

37. Tufts, "A Social Philosopher's Idea of Good Government," 194.

38. Mary Parker Follett, *The New State: Group Organization the Solution of Popular Government*, 368.

39. Tufts and Dewey, *Ethics* (MW 5:74).

40. Paul Goodman, *Utopian Essays and Practical Proposals*, 21.

41. Cf. Hayek: "The opportunities open to the poor in a competitive society are much more restricted than those open to the rich" (*The Road to Serfdom*, 102; cf. Adam Smith, *Lectures on Jurisprudence*, 512).

42. Tufts, "A Social Philosopher's Idea of Good Government," 195.

43. See Hirsch, *Social Limits to Growth*, 162–63 n.2; Hayek, *The Constitution of Liberty*, 91–93.

44. Niebuhr, *Moral Man and Immoral Society*, 4.

45. A similar position has more recently been expressed by Glenn Tinder: "Man is not capable of community—not, at least, in any full and stable form" (*Community: Reflections on a Tragic Ideal*, 2).

46. Niebuhr, *Moral Man and Immoral Society*, 22; cf. 219.

Chapter 7. Optimism, Meliorism, Faith

1. J. Hector St. John de Crèvecoeur, *Letters from an American Farmer*, 137; Arthur A. Ekirch, Jr., *The Idea of Progress in America, 1815–60*, 11.

2. John E. Smith, *Purpose and Thought: The Meaning of Pragmatism*, 120; Henry F. May, *The End of American Innocence*, 24. On progress in America, see also Boyd C. Shafer, "The American Heritage of Hope, 1865–1940," 427–50; Rush Welter, "The Idea of Progress in America," 401–15; Chambers, "The Belief in Progress in Twentieth-Century America," 197–224; David W. Marcell, *Progress and Pragmatism; James, Dewey, Beard, and the American Idea of Progress*.

3. Frederick Jackson Turner, *The Frontier in American History*, 2, 259–60.

4. For a reexamination of Turner's frontier thesis, see Curti, "Frederick Jackson Turner, 1861–1932" in *Probing Our Past*, 32–55; Henry Nash Smith, *Virgin Land: The American West as Symbol and Myth;* Lee Benson, "The Historical Background to Turner's Frontier Essay," 59–82; George R. Taylor, ed., *The*

Turner Thesis; Ellen von Nardroff, "The American Frontier as a Safety Valve—The Life, Death, Reincarnation, and Justification of a Theory," 123–42; Ray Alan Billington, *Frederick Jackson Turner.*

5. Roosevelt, *Public Papers and Addresses,* 1:749–50, 756. For Roosevelt's reworking of the frontier thesis, see Curtis Nettels, "Frederick Jackson Turner and the New Deal," 257–65; Steven Kesselman, "The Frontier Thesis and the Great Depression," 253–68. See also Walter Prescott Webb, *Divided We Stand: The Crisis of a Frontierless Democracy.*

6. Lester Frank Ward, *Dynamic Sociology,* 1:35; Chambers, "The Belief in Progress in Twentieth-Century America," 198; Walter E. Weyl, *The New Democracy,* 166.

7. George Bancroft, "The Office of the People in Art, Government, and Religion," 113; Carl Sandburg, "The People, Yes," [1936], in *The Complete Poems of Carl Sandburg,* 615; Walt Whitman, *Democratic Vistas* [1871], in *The Portable Walt Whitman,* 340.

8. Thomas Vernor Smith, *The American Philosophy of Equality,* 202–3; Santayana, *The Life of Reason, or The Phases of Human Progress,* 1:190; Randolph Bourne, "Twilight of Idols," in *The World of Randolph Bourne,* 203.

9. From *The Complete Works of Ralph Waldo Emerson:* "Fate," 6:6; *Nature,* 1:40; "Fate," 6:35; "The Sovereignty of Ethics," 10:188.

10. Ibid.: "Compensation," 2:96, 98; "Considerations by the Way," 6:252; "Emancipation in the British West Indies," 11:147; "Compensation," 2:119.

11. Ibid.: "Spiritual Laws," 2:135. For a series of very different views of Emerson's optimism, see Mildred Silver, "Emerson and the Idea of Progress," 1–19; Stephen E. Whicher, *Freedom and Fate: An Inner Life of Ralph Waldo Emerson;* McDermott, *Streams of Experience: Reflections on the History and Philosophy of American Culture,* 29–43; Robert C. Pollock, "Emerson and America's Future," 48–74.

12. See Dewey, MW 4:8; MW 15:63–64; LW 5:115; LW 11:42–43; LW 13:178, 187.

13. See MW 2:315; LW 3:105.

14. See Mead, MT 292–94; PA 466–78; SW 264–66.

15. See Mead, MSS 248–52; MT 168, 261; PA 489–90.

16. See Mead, MSS 294; Mead, "The Working Hypothesis in Social Reform," 368.

17. See Mead, SW 248–66; Mead, "Bishop Berkeley and His Message," 430.

18. Mead, "Bishop Berkeley and His Message," 430.

19. May Brodbeck, "The Philosophy of John Dewey," 215.

20. Asher Moore, "The Promised Land," 187–88.

21. Pfuetze, *Self, Society, Existence,* 269; Niebuhr, *Moral Man and Immoral Society,* 35, 3. Cf. Niebuhr, *The Irony of American History,* 82.

22. Niebuhr, *The Nature and Destiny of Man.* Vol. 1: *Human Nature,* 111; cf. Niebuhr, "The Blindness of Liberalism," 4–5.

23. McGill, "Pragmatism Reconsidered: An Aspect of John Dewey's Philosophy," 291; Edwin A. Burtt, "The Core of Dewey's Way of Thinking," 418; Pfuetze, *Self, Society, Existence,* 238.

24. Krutch, *The Measure of Man*, 25.

25. Niebuhr, *The Irony of American History*, 81.

26. Howard B. White, "The Political Faith of John Dewey," 361.

27. John Herman Randall, Jr., "Dewey's Contribution to Scientific Humanism," 136. Cf. Thomas Vernor Smith, "The Social Philosophy of George Herbert Mead," 380; McDermott, *Streams of Experience*, 92–106.

28. Randall, "The Spirit of American Philosophy," 128.

29. James, *The Will to Believe*, 79, 29; cf. 80–89.

30. Thomas Vernor Smith, "The Social Philosophy of George Herbert Mead," 380; Howard B. White, "The Political Faith of John Dewey," 366–67.

31. See Dewey, LW 5:267–68; LW 9:14–15.

32. Niebuhr, "The Blindness of Liberalism"; Georges Dicker, "John Dewey: Instrumentalism in Social Action," 225.

33. Dicker, "John Dewey: Instrumentalism in Social Action," 225.

34. Cf. Dewey, MW 14:184; LW 1:313–15; LW 9:50–51.

35. See Dewey, LW 9:54; LW 15:55–62; Van Meter Ames, "Buber and Mead," 181–82.

36. James, *The Will to Believe*, 25.

37. Cf. Mead, MSS 167–68, 199, 265, 386.

38. Sandburg, *The People, Yes*, 462. Cf. Sandburg, *Remembrance Rock*.

Chapter 8. Philosophers and the Nature of Wisdom

1. Otto, "Philosophy in the Community," 279.

2. From among the many discussions of professional philosophy, consider Paul T. Durbin, "The 'Professionalization' of Philosophy: An Essay in the Sociology of Philosophy," 98–109; Alison Jagger, "Philosophy as a Profession," 100–116; Edward Regis, Jr., "The Layman and the Abdication of Philosophers," 117–26; Bruce Kuklick, *The Rise of American Philosophy;* Edward I. Pitts, "The Profession of Philosophy in America."

3. For example, my own twenty-four-thousand-student component of the state university system of Ohio was founded in 1872 as a municipal institution "for the promotion of practical education" under the name of the Toledo University of Arts and Trades. See Frank R. Hickerson, *The Tower Builders*, 433–34.

4. James, *Essays, Comments, and Reviews*, 67–74.

5. Berry, *Home Economics*, 77, 86.

6. Berry, *Standing by Words*, 4.

7. Berry, *The Unsettling of America*, 21.

8. Archibald MacLeish's attack on the intellectuals' failure to actively oppose the rise of fascism is contained in "The Irresponsibles" in *A Time to Speak*, 103–21. The passages cited appear on pp. 113, 115, 116, 117, 118, 114, 116.

9. MacLeish continues that the writer, on the other hand, aims at writing "with such skill, such penetration of the physical presence of the world, that the action seen, the action described, will 'really happen' on his page." This isolating focus is possible only because the writer had come to see the world

"as a god sees it—without morality, without care, without judgment." And the justification for adopting this distance was the belief that "the artist's obligations are obligations to his art. His responsibility—his one responsibility—is to his art" (ibid., 119–20).

10. Curti, "Intellectuals and Other People," 279.

11. Murphy, "Pronouncements, Propaganda, and Philosophy," in *Reason and the Common Good: Selected Essays of A. E. Murphy*, 376–84. The passages cited appear on pp. 378, 379, 383. See also Murphy, "The Professional Philosopher," 69–86, and "Problems of Men," 194–202.

12. Brodbeck, "Philosophy in America, 1900–50," 59, 61, 93.

13. Blandshard, "Can the Philosopher Influence Social Change?," 751, 750, 752, and 750.

14. Cf. Dewey, LW 16:319, 365, 389.

15. Rorty, *Philosophy and the Mirror of Nature*, 162.

16. Rorty, *Consequences of Pragmatism*, 62.

17. See ibid., 221.

18. Rorty, *Philosophy and the Mirror of Nature*, 378.

19. Rorty, *Consequences of Pragmatism*, 172.

20. Rorty, *Philosophy and the Mirror of Nature*, 12; cf. 360.

21. Ibid., 166; Rorty, *Consequences of Pragmatism*, 218.

22. McDermott, *Streams of Experience*, 96–97.

23. Rorty, *Consequences of Pragmatism*, 87.

24. Ibid., 64. For a further elaboration of this interpretation of Rorty's Pragmatism, see my "Rorty's Use of Dewey."

25. Otto, "Philosophy in the Community," 298; see also Otto, "Philosophy in a Time of Social Crisis," 293–301.

26. Mead, "The Philosophy of John Dewey," 66, 68.

27. Tufts, "Dr. Angell, the New President of Yale," 400.

WORKS CITED

Addams, Jane. "Ethical Survivals in Municipal Corruption." *International Journal of Ethics* 8 (April 1898): 273–91.

Ames, Van Meter. "Buber and Mead." *Antioch Review* 27 (1967): 181–91.

Axtelle, George E., and Joe R. Burnett. "Dewey on Education and Schooling." In *Guide to the Works of John Dewey,* edited by Jo Ann Boydston, 257–305. Carbondale: Southern Illinois University Press, 1970.

Ayres, Clarence E. "Philosophy and Genius." *Ethics* 40 (January 1930): 263–71.

Bancroft, George. "The Office of the People in Art, Government, and Religion" [1855]. In *American Philosophic Addresses, 1700–1900,* edited by Joseph L. Blau, 98–114. New York: Columbia University Press, 1946.

Beard, Charles A. *The Republic: Conversations on Fundamentals.* New York: Viking, 1944.

Beard, Charles A., and Mary R. Beard. *America in Midpassage.* New York: Macmillan, 1939.

Becker, Carl. "New Liberties for Old." *Journal of Social Philosophy* 1 (January 1936): 101–21.

Bellah, Robert N., Richard Madsen, William M. Sullivan, Ann Swindler, and Steven M. Tipton. *Habits of the Heart: Individualism and Commitment in American Life.* Berkeley: University of California Press, 1985.

Benda, Julien. "The Attack on Western Morality." *Commentary* 4 (November 1947): 416–22.

Benson, Lee. "The Historical Background to Turner's Frontier Essay." *Agricultural History* 25 (1951): 59–82.

Berry, Wendell. *A Continuous Harmony.* New York: Harcourt, Brace, Jovanovich, 1970.

———. *The Hidden Wound.* Boston: Houghton Mifflin, 1970.

———. *The Unsettling of America: Culture and Agriculture.* San Francisco: Sierra Club Books, 1977.

———. *The Gift of Good Land.* San Francisco: North Point Press, 1981.

———. *Standing by Words.* San Francisco: North Point Press, 1983.

————. *Home Economics*. San Francisco: North Point Press, 1987.

Bhattacharya, N.C. "Demythologizing John Dewey." *Journal of Educational Thought* 8 (December 1974): 117–23.

Billington, Ray Alan. *Frederick Jackson Turner*. New York: Oxford University Press, 1973.

Blanshard, Brand. "Can the Philosopher Influence Social Change?" *Journal of Philosophy* 51 (November 25, 1954): 741–53.

Blanshard, Brand, Curt J. Ducasse, Arthur E. Murphy, Max C. Otto, and Charles W. Hendel, eds. *Philosophy in American Education: Its Tasks and Opportunities*. New York: Harper & Bros., 1945.

Blau, Joseph L. *Men and Movements in American Philosophy*. Englewood Cliffs, N.J.: Prentice-Hall, 1952.

Bordeau, Edward J. "Dewey's Ideas about the Great Depression." *Journal of the History of Ideas* 32 (January-March 1971): 67–84.

Bourne, Randolph. *The World of Randolph Bourne*, edited by Lillian Schlissel. New York: Dutton, 1965.

Brickman, William H. "Dewey's Social and Political Commentary." *Guide to the Works of John Dewey*, edited by Jo Ann Boydston, 218–56. Carbondale: Southern Illinois University Press, 1970.

Brodbeck, May. "The Philosophy of John Dewey." In *Essays in Ontology*, 188–215. Iowa Publications in Philosophy, vol. 1. Iowa City: University of Iowa Press, 1963.

Brodbeck, May, James Gray, and Walter Metzger, eds. *American Nonfiction, 1900–50*. Chicago: Regnery, 1952.

Brown, Richard J. "John Dewey and the League for Independent Political Action." *Social Studies* 59 (April 1968): 156–61.

Buchler, Justus. *Charles Peirce's Empiricism*. New York: Harcourt, Brace, 1939.

————. *The Concept of Method*. New York: Columbia University Press, 1961.

Burke, Kenneth. "Liberalism's Family Tree." *New Republic*, March 4, 1936, 115–16.

————. "George Herbert Mead." *New Republic*, January 11, 1939, 292–93.

Burtt, Edwin A. "The Core of Dewey's Way of Thinking." *Journal of Philosophy* 57 (June 23, 1960): 401–19.

Campbell, James. "Rorty's Use of Dewey." *Southern Journal of Philosophy* 22 (Summer 1984): 175–87.

————. "George Herbert Mead: Philosophy and the Pragmatic Self." In *American Philosophy*, edited by Marcus G. Singer, 91–114. Cambridge: Cambridge University Press, 1985.

————. Introduction to *Selected Writings of James Hayden Tufts*, edited by James Campbell. Carbondale: Southern Illinois University Press, 1992.

————. "Ayer and Pragmatism." In *The Philosophy of A. J. Ayer*, edited by Lewis E. Hahn. LaSalle: Open Court, 1991.

Chambers, Clarke A. "The Belief in Progress in Twentieth-Century America." *Journal of the History of Ideas* 19 (1958): 197–224.

————. *Seedtime of Reform: American Social Service and Social Action, 1918–33*. Ann Arbor: University of Michigan Press, 1967.

Cohen, Morris R. "Some Difficulties in Dewey's Anthropocentric Naturalism." *Philosophical Review* 49 (March 1940): 196–228.

———. *A Preface to Logic.* New York: Holt, 1944.

———. *American Thought: A Critical Sketch.* Glencoe, Ill.: Free Press, 1954.

Cooley, Charles Horton. *Human Nature and the Social Order.* New York: Scribners, 1912.

———. *Social Organization.* New York: Scribners, 1916.

Crèvecoeur, J. Hector St. John de. *Letters from an American Farmer.* New York: Dutton, [1782] 1957.

Curti, Merle E. "Intellectuals and Other People." *American Historical Review* 60 (January 1955): 259–82.

———. *Probing Our Past.* New York: Harper & Bros., 1955.

———. *The Social Ideas of American Educators.* Paterson, N.J.: Littlefield, Adams & Co., 1959.

———. *Human Nature in American Thought: A History.* Madison: University of Wisconsin Press, 1980.

Dewey, John. *The Early Works of John Dewey, 1882–98,* edited by Jo Ann Boydston. Critical Edition. 5 vols. Carbondale: Southern Illinois University Press, 1969–72.

———. *The Middle Works of John Dewey, 1899–1924,* edited by Jo Ann Boydston. Critical Edition. 15 vols. Carbondale: Southern Illinois University Press, 1976–83.

———. *The Later Works of John Dewey, 1925–53,* edited by Jo Ann Boydston. Critical Edition. 17 vols. and a one-volume cumulative index. Carbondale: Southern Illinois University Press, 1981– .

Dicker, Georges. "John Dewey: Instrumentalism in Social Action." *Transactions of the Charles S. Peirce Society* 7 (1971): 221–32.

Durbin, Paul T. "The 'Professionalization' of Philosophy: An Essay in the Sociology of Philosophy." *Proceedings of the American Catholic Philosophical Association* 47 (1973): 98–109.

Dykhuizen, George. *The Life and Mind of John Dewey.* Carbondale: Southern Illinois University Press, 1973.

Eames, S. Morris. *Pragmatic Naturalism: An Introduction.* Carbondale: Southern Illinois University Press, 1977.

Edel, Abraham. "Notes on the Search for a Moral Philosophy in William James." In *The Philosophy of William James,* edited by W. R. Corti, 245–60. Hamburg: Felix Meiner, 1976.

Edman, Irwin. *Philosopher's Holiday.* New York: Viking, 1938.

Ekirch, Arthur A., Jr. *The Idea of Progress in America, 1815–60.* New York: Columbia University Press, 1944.

Emerson, Ralph Waldo. *The Complete Works of Ralph Waldo Emerson,* edited by Edward Waldo Emerson. 12 vols. Boston: Houghton, Mifflin, 1904.

———. *Journals and Miscellaneous Notebooks of Ralph Waldo Emerson,* edited by William H. Gilman et al. 16 vols. Cambridge, Mass.: Harvard University Press, 1960–82.

Feinberg, Walter. "The Conflict between Intelligence and Community in Dewey's Educational Philosophy." *Educational Theory* 19 (Summer 1969): 236–48.

Fisch, Max H. *Peirce, Semeiotic, and Pragmatism,* edited by K. L. Ketner and C. J. W. Kloessel. Bloomington: Indiana University Press, 1986.

Flower, Elizabeth, and Murray G. Murphey. *A History of Philosophy in America.* 2 vols. New York: Putnam's, 1977.

Follett, Mary Parker. *The New State: Group Organization the Solution of Popular Government.* New York: Longmans, Green, 1923.

Foster, William Zebulon. *Toward Soviet America.* New York: Coward-McCann, 1932.

Frankel, Charles. "John Dewey's Legacy." *American Scholar* 29 (Summer 1960): 313–31.

———. "John Dewey's Social Philosophy." In *New Studies in the Philosophy of John Dewey,* edited by Steven M. Cahn, 3–44. Hanover, N.H.: University Press of New England, 1977.

Garrison, George R., and Edward H. Madden. "William James—Warts and All." *American Quarterly* 29 (Summer 1977): 207–21.

Goodman, Paul. *Utopian Essays and Practical Proposals.* New York: Vintage, 1962.

Grimes, Alan P. *American Political Thought,* rev. ed. New York: Holt, Rinehart & Winston, 1960.

Gouinlock, James. "Philosophy and Moral Values: The Pragmatic Analysis." In *Pragmatism: Its Sources and Prospects,* edited by Robert J. Mulvaney and Philip M. Zeltner, 99–119. Columbia: University of South Carolina Press, 1981.

Hayek, Friedrich A. *The Road to Serfdom.* Chicago: University of Chicago Press, 1944.

———. *The Constitution of Liberty.* Chicago: University of Chicago Press, 1960.

Hickerson, Frank R. *The Tower Builders.* Toledo: University of Toledo Press, 1972.

Hirsch, Fred. *Social Limits of Growth.* Cambridge, Mass.: Harvard University Press, 1976.

Hocking, William Ernest. "Action and Certainty." 1930. Reprinted in *Dewey and His Critics,* edited by S. Morgenbesser, 19–32. New York: *Journal of Philosophy,* 1977.

Hofstadter, Richard. *Anti–intellectualism in American Life.* New York: Vintage, 1963.

Holmes, Oliver Wendell, Jr. *Towne v. Eisner,* 245 U.S. 418–27 (1917).

Hook, Sidney. *Pragmatism and the Tragic Sense of Life.* New York: Basic Books, 1974.

Hoover, Herbert. *American Individualism.* Garden City, N.J.: Doubleday, Page, 1923.

———. *The Challenge to Liberty.* New York: Scribners, 1934.

Jagger, Alison. "Philosophy as a Profession." *Metaphilosophy* 6 (January 1975): 100–16.

James, Alice. *The Diary of Alice James,* edited by Leon Edel. New York: Dodd, Mead, & Co., 1964.

James, William. *Essays, Comments, and Reviews*. Cambridge, Mass.: Harvard University Press, 1987. (This work, and the ones following that are published by Harvard University Press, are part of the Works of William James Series.)

———. *Essays in Philosophy*. Cambridge, Mass.: Harvard University Press, 1978.

———. *Essays in Religion and Morality*. Cambridge, Mass.: Harvard University Press, 1982.

———. *The Letters of William James*, edited by Henry James, Jr. 2 vols. Boston: Atlantic Monthly Press, 1920.

———. *The Meaning of Truth: A Sequel to 'Pragmatism'*. Cambridge, Mass.: Harvard University Press, [1909] 1975.

———. *A Pluralistic Universe*. Cambridge, Mass.: Harvard University Press, [1909] 1977.

———. *Pragmatism: A New Name for Some Old Ways of Thinking*. Cambridge, Mass.: Harvard University Press, [1907] 1975.

———. *The Principles of Psychology*. Cambridge, Mass.: Harvard University Press, [1890] 1981.

———. *Talks to Teachers on Psychology and to Students on Some of Life's Ideals*. Cambridge, Mass.: Harvard University Press, [1899] 1983.

———. *The Varieties of Religious Experience*. Cambridge, Mass.: Harvard University Press, [1902] 1985.

———. *The Will to Believe and Other Essays in Popular Philosophy*. Cambridge, Mass.: Harvard University Press, [1897] 1979.

Kaplan, Sidney. "Social Engineers as Saviors: Effects of WWI on Some American Liberals." *Journal of the History of Ideas* 17 (June 1956): 347–69.

Karier, Clarence. "Making the World Safe for Democracy: An Historical Critique of John Dewey's Pragmatic Liberal Philosophy in the Warfare State." *Educational Theory* 27 (Winter 1977): 12–47.

Kesselman, Steven. "The Frontier Thesis and the Great Depression." *Journal of the History of Ideas* 29 (1968): 253–68.

Kirk, Russell. *The Conservative Mind: From Burke to Eliot*. 6th rev. ed. South Bend, Ind.: Gateway Editions, 1978.

Kuklick, Bruce. *The Rise of American Philosophy*. New Haven, Conn.: Yale University Press, 1977.

Krutch, Joseph Wood. *The Measure of Man*. 1952. Reprint. Indianapolis: Bobbs-Merrill, 1962.

Lamont, Corliss. "New Light on Dewey's *Common Faith*." *Journal of Philosophy* 58 (January 5, 1961): 22–25.

Levi, Albert W. *Philosophy and the Modern World*. Bloomington: Indiana University Press, 1959.

Lilienthal, David E. *TVA: Democracy on the March*. New York: Harper & Bros., 1944.

Lincoln, Abraham. *The Collected Works of Abraham Lincoln*, edited by Roy P. Basler. 8 vols. New Brunswick, N.J.: Rutgers University Press, 1953.

Lippmann, Walter, *A Preface to Politics*. New York: Mitchell Kennerley, 1913.

———. *Drift and Mastery: An Attempt to Diagnose the Current Unrest*. New York: Mitchell Kennerley, 1914.

———. *The Public Philosophy*. New York: New American Library, 1955.

Locke, John. *The Second Treatise of Government*. 1690. In *Two Treatises of Government*, edited by Peter Laslett. Cambridge: Cambridge University Press, 1960.

MacLeish, Archibald. *A Time to Speak*. Boston: Houghton-Mifflin, 1941.

Madden, Edward H. *Chauncey Wright and the Foundations of Pragmatism*. Seattle: University of Washington Press, 1963.

———. *Chauncey Wright*. New York: Washington Square Press, 1964.

Manicas, Peter T. *The Death of the State*. New York: Capricorn, 1974.

Marcell, David W. *Progress and Pragmatism: James, Dewey, Beard, and the American Idea of Progress*. Westport, Conn.: Greenwood Press, 1974.

May, Henry F. *The End of American Innocence*. Chicago: Quadrangle, 1964.

McClellan, James E. "Dewey and the Concept of Method: Quest for the Philosopher's Stone in Education." *School Review* 67 (Summer 1959): 213–28.

McDermott, John J. "A Metaphysics of Relations: James' Anticipation of Contemporary Experience." In *The Philosophy of William James*, edited by W. R. Corti, 81–99. Hamburg: Felix Meiner, 1976.

———. *Streams of Experience: Reflections on the History and Philosophy of American Culture*. Amherst: University of Massachusetts Press, 1986.

McGill, Vivian J. "Pragmatism Reconsidered: An Aspect of John Dewey's Philosophy." *Science & Society* 3 (Summer 1939): 289–322.

Mead, George Herbert. "The Working Hypothesis in Social Reform." *American Journal of Sociology* 5 (1899): 367–71.

———. Review of Gustave Le Bon, *The Psychology of Socialism*. *American Journal of Sociology* 5 (1899): 404–12.

———. Review of Jane Addams, *The Newer Ideals of Peace*. *American Journal of Sociology* 13 (1907): 121–28.

———. "The Social Settlement: Its Basis and Function." *University* [of Chicago] *Record* 12 (1908): 108–10.

———. *The Conscientious Objector*. New York: National Security League, 1918.

———. Review of Thorstein Veblen, *The Nature of Peace and the Terms of Its Perpetuation*. *Journal of Political Economy* 26 (1918): 752–62.

———. "Bishop Berkeley and His Message." *Journal of Philosophy* 26 (1929): 421–30.

———. "National-Mindedness and International-Mindedness." *International Journal of Ethics* 39 (July 1929): 385–407.

———. *The Philosophy of the Present*, edited by Arthur E. Murphy. Chicago: University of Chicago Press, [1932] 1980.

———. *Mind, Self, and Society from the Standpoint of a Social Behaviorist*, edited by Charles W. Morris. Chicago: University of Chicago Press, [1934] 1967.

———. "The Philosophy of John Dewey." *International Journal of Ethics* 46 (1935): 64–81.

———. *Movements of Thought in the Nineteenth Century*, edited by Merritt H. Moore. Chicago: University of Chicago Press, [1936] 1972.

———. *The Philosophy of the Act*, edited by Charles W. Morris, John M. Brewster, Albert M. Dunham, and David L. Miller. Chicago: University of Chicago Press, [1938] 1972.

———. *Selected Writings,* edited by Andrew J. Reck. Chicago: University of Chicago Press, [1964] 1981.

Mencken, H. L. *Notes on Democracy.* New York: Knopf, 1926.

Metz, Joseph G. "Democracy and the Scientific Method in the Philosophy of John Dewey." *Review of Politics* 31 (April 1969): 242–62.

Miller, David L. *George Herbert Mead: Self, Language and the World.* 1973. Reprint. Chicago: University of Chicago Press, 1980.

Mills, C. Wright. *The Power Elite.* New York: Oxford University Press, 1956.

———. *Sociology and Pragmatism: The Higher Learning in America,* edited by I. L. Horowitz. New York: Oxford University Press, 1964.

Moore, Asher. "The Promised Land." *Monist* 57 (April 1973): 176–90.

Murphy, Arthur E. "The Professional Philosopher." In *Philosophy in American Education: Its Tasks and Opportunities,* edited by Brand Blanshard et al., 69–86. New York: Harper & Bros., 1945.

———. "Problems of Men." *Philosophical Review* 56 (1947): 194–202.

———. "Philosophical Scholarship." In *American Scholarship in the Twentieth Century,* edited by Merle E. Curti, 168–206. Cambridge, Mass.: Harvard University Press, 1953.

———. *Reason and the Common Good: Selected Essays of A. E. Murphy,* edited by W. H. Hay, M. G. Singer, and A. E. Murphy, 367–84. Englewood Cliffs, N.J.: Prentice-Hall, 1963.

von Nardroff, Ellen. "The American Frontier as a Safety Valve—The Life, Death, Reincarnation, and Justification of a Theory." *Agricultural History* 36 (July 1962): 123–42.

Nettels, Curtis. "Frederick Jackson Turner and the New Deal." *Wisconsin Magazine of History* 17 (1934): 257–65.

Niebuhr, Reinhold. *Leaves from the Notebook of a Tamed Cynic.* San Francisco: Harper & Row, [1929] 1980.

———. *Moral Man and Immoral Society: A Study in Ethics and Politics.* New York: Scribners, [1932] 1960.

———. "The Blindness of Liberalism." *Radical Religion* 1 (1936): 4–5.

———. *The Nature and Destiny of Man.* Vol. 1: *Human Nature.* New York: Scribners, [1941] 1964.

———. *The Irony of American History.* New York: Scribners, 1962.

Nozick, Robert. *Anarchy, State, and Utopia.* New York: Basic Books, 1974.

Otto, Max C. "Philosophy in a Time of Social Crisis." *Journal of Social Philosophy* 6 (July 1941): 293–301.

———. "On a Certain Blindness in William James." *Ethics* 53 (April 1943): 184–91.

———. "Philosophy in the Community." In *Philosophy in American Education: Its Tasks and Opportunities,* edited by Brand Blanshard et al., 279–98. New York: Harper & Bros., 1945.

Parrington, Vernon Louis, Jr. "Vernon Parrington's View: Economics and Criticism." *Pacific Northwest Quarterly* 44 (July 1953): 97–105.

Peirce, Charles Sanders. *The Collected Papers of Charles Sanders Peirce,* edited by Charles Hartshorne, Paul Weiss, and Arthur W. Burks. 8 vols. Cambridge, Mass.: Harvard University Press, 1931–58.

Perry, Ralph Barton. *Puritanism and Democracy*. New York: Vanguard, 1944.
———, ed. *The Thought and Character of William James*. 2 vols. Boston: Little, Brown, 1935.
Pfuetze, Paul E. *Self, Society, Existence: Human Nature and Dialogue in the Thought of George Herbert Mead and Martin Buber*. New York: Harper Torchbooks, 1961.
Pitts, Edward I. "The Profession of Philosophy in America." Ph.D. diss., Pennsylvania State University, 1979.
Pollock, Robert C. "Emerson and America's Future." In *Doctrine and Experience: Essays in American Philosophy*, edited by Vincent G. Potter, 48–74. New York: Fordham University Press, 1988.
Randall, John Herman, Jr. "The Spirit of American Philosophy." In *Wellsprings of the American Spirit*, edited by F. E. Johnson, 117–33. New York: Institute for Religious and Social Studies, 1948.
———. "Dewey's Contribution to Scientific Humanism." *Humanist* 19 (1959): 134–38.
Ratner, Joseph. Editor's note on the Outlawry of War movement. In *Intelligence in the Modern World: John Dewey's Philosophy*, edited by Joseph Ratner, 525–66. New York: Modern Library, 1939.
Regis, Edward, Jr. "The Layman and the Abdication of Philosophers." *Metaphilosophy* 6 (January 1975): 117–26.
Roosevelt, Franklin Delano. *The Public Papers and Addresses of Franklin Delano Roosevelt*, edited by Samuel I. Rosenman. 13 vols. New York: Random House, 1938–50.
Rorty, Richard. *Philosophy and the Mirror of Nature*. Princeton, N.J.: Princeton University Press, 1979.
———. *Consequences of Pragmatism*. Minneapolis: University of Minnesota Press, 1982.
Royce, Josiah. *William James and Other Essays on the Philosophy of Life*. New York: Macmillan, 1912.
Rucker, Darnell. *The Chicago Pragmatists*. Minneapolis: University of Minnesota Press, 1969.
Sabine, George H. "The Pragmatic Approach to Politics." *American Political Science Review* 24 (November 1930): 865–85.
Sandburg, Carl. *Remembrance Rock*. New York: Harcourt, Brace & World, 1948.
———. *The Complete Poems of Carl Sandburg*. New York: Harcourt, Brace, Jovanovich, 1976.
Santayana, George. *The Life of Reason, or The Phases of Human Progress*. 5 vols. London: Constable, 1905.
———. *Character and Opinion in the United States*. New York: Scribners, 1920.
Schlesinger, Arthur M., Jr. "Reinhold Niebuhr's Role in American Political Thought and Life." In *Reinhold Niebuhr: His Religious, Social, and Political Thought*, edited by Charles W. Kegley and Robert W. Bretall, 126–50. New York: Macmillan, 1961.
Schneider, Herbert W. *A History of American Philosophy*. 2d ed. New York: Columbia University Press, 1963.

Shafer, Boyd C. "The American Heritage of Hope, 1865–1940." *Mississippi Valley Historical Review* 37 (1950): 427–50.

Sheldon, Wilmon H. "Professor Dewey, The Protagonist of Democracy." *Journal of Philosophy* 18 (June 9, 1921): 309–20.

Silver, Mildred. "Emerson and the Idea of Progress." *American Literature* 12 (1940): 1–19.

Sleeper, Ralph W. *The Necessity of Pragmatism: John Dewey's Conception of Philosophy.* New Haven, Conn.: Yale University Press, 1986.

Smith, Adam. *The Theory of Moral Sentiments,* edited by D. D. Raphael et al. Oxford: Clarendon Press, [1759] 1979.

———. *Lectures on Jurisprudence,* edited by R. L. Meeks et al. Oxford: Clarendon Press, [1762–66] 1978.

———. *An Inquiry into the Nature and Causes of the Wealth of Nations,* edited by R. H. Campbell et al. Oxford: Clarendon Press, [1776] 1979.

Smith, Henry Nash. *Virgin Land: The American West as Symbol and Myth.* Cambridge, Mass.: Harvard University Press, 1950.

Smith, John E. *Purpose and Thought: The Meaning of Pragmatism.* New Haven, Conn.: Yale University Press, 1978.

———. *The Spirit of American Philosophy.* Rev. ed. Albany: State University of New York Press, 1983.

Smith, Thomas Vernor. *The American Philosophy of Equality.* Chicago: University of Chicago Press, 1927.

———. *The Philosophic Way of Life.* Chicago: University of Chicago Press, 1929.

———. "The Social Philosophy of George Herbert Mead." *American Journal of Sociology* 37 (1931): 368–85.

Suckiel, Ellen Kappy. *The Pragmatic Philosophy of William James.* Notre Dame, Ind.: University of Notre Dame Press, 1982.

Sumner, William Graham. *The Challenge of Facts and Other Essays,* edited by Albert Galloway Keller. New Haven, Conn.: Yale University Press, 1914.

———. *The Forgotten Man and Other Essays,* edited by Albert Galloway Keller. New Haven, Conn.: Yale University Press, 1918.

Taylor, George R., ed. *The Turner Thesis.* Boston: Heath, 1956.

Thayer, H. S. *Meaning and Action: A Critical History of Pragmatism.* Rev. ed. Indianapolis: Hackett, 1981.

Thoreau, Henry David. *Walden,* edited by J. Lyndon Shanley. Princeton, N.J.: Princeton University Press, [1854] 1971.

———. *Reform Papers,* edited by Wendell Glick. Princeton, N.J.: Princeton University Press, 1973.

Thorndike, Edward Lee. "The Psychology of the Half-Educated Man." *Harper's Magazine* 140 (1920): 666–70.

Tinder, Glenn. *Community: Reflections on a Tragic Ideal.* Baton Rouge: Louisiana State University Press, 1980.

Tufts, James Hayden. "The University and the Advance of Justice." *University of Chicago Magazine* 5 (April 1913): 186–98.

———. "The Present Significance of Scholarship." *Washington University Record* 10 (December 1914): 1–12.

———. "The Community and Economic Groups." *Philosophical Review* 28 (November 1919): 589–97.

———. "Dr. Angell, the New President of Yale." *The World's Work* 42 (August 1921): 387–400.

———. "A Social Philosopher's Idea of Good Government." *Annals of the American Academy of Political and Social Science* 169 (September 1933): 193–201.

———. "The Institution as Agency of Stability and Readjustment in Ethics." *Philosophical Review* 44 (March 1935): 138–53.

———. *Selected Writings of James Hayden Tufts*, edited by James Campbell. Carbondale: Southern Illinois University Press, 1992.

Tufts, James Hayden, and John Dewey. *Ethics*. The 1908 edition appears as volume 5 of *The Middle Works of John Dewey;* the revised 1932 edition appears as volume 7 of *The Later Works of John Dewey*.

Turner, Frederick Jackson. *The Frontier in American History*. New York: Holt, Rinehart & Winston, [1920] 1962.

Veblen, Thorstein. *The Theory of the Leisure Class*. New York: New American Library, [1899] 1953.

Ward, Lester Frank. *Dynamic Sociology or Applied Social Science as Based upon Statistical Sociology and the Less Complex Sciences*. 2 vols. 1883. Reprint. New York: Dutton, 1920.

Webb, Walter Prescott. *Divided We Stand: The Crisis of a Frontierless Democracy*. New York: Farrar and Rinehart, 1937.

Welter, Rush. "The Idea of Progress in America." *Journal of the History of Ideas* 16 (1955): 401–15.

Weyl, Walter E. *The New Democracy*. New York: Macmillan, 1913.

Whicher, Stephen E. *Freedom and Fate: An Inner Life of Ralph Waldo Emerson*. Philadelphia: University of Pennsylvania Press, 1953.

White, Howard B. "The Political Faith of John Dewey." *The Journal of Politics* 20 (1958): 353–67.

White, Morton G. *Social Thought in America: The Revolt against Formalism*. Rev. ed. Boston: Beacon Press, 1957.

———. *Science and Sentiment in America*. New York: Oxford University Press, 1972.

Whitman, Walt. *The Portable Walt Whitman*, edited by Mark Van Doren. New York: Viking Press, 1973.

Wiener, Philip P. *Evolution and the Founders of Pragmatism*. Cambridge, Mass.: Harvard University Press, 1949.

Wild, John. *The Radical Empiricism of William James*. New York: Anchor, 1970.

INDEX

Addams, Jane, 125n.18

Bancroft, George, 93
Becker, Carl, 73–74, 82
Bellah, Robert N., 79
Berry, Wendell: on the responsibilities of intellectuals, 112, 116, 119; on self-discipline, 78–79
Blanshard, Brand: on philosophy and social reform, 115, 116, 126n.13
Bourne, Randolph, 93
Brodbeck, May: on the nature of philosophy, 114–15, 116; on optimism, 97
Buchler, Justus, 43
Burke, Kenneth, 27

Chambers, Clarke A., 92
Community: nature and importance of, 8, 33–35, 57–58, 87–88, 109, 120
Conceptual reconstruction: concepts as tools, 53, 54, 63, 65, 69–70, 128n.14; as an ongoing necessity, 7, 8, 52–55, 59–70
Cooley, Charles Horton, 62
Cooperative inquiry, 3, 9, 42–43, 58, 103–4
Crèvecoeur, J. Hector St. John de, 91
Curti, Merle E.: on intellectuals and social problems, 113; on the meaning of "human nature," 128n.14; on James, 16

Democracy: criticisms of, 23–24, 36, 48–49, 76, 89–90, 97–99; and experts, 46, 48–52; nature of, 8, 56–58, 66–68, 71–72, 85–90, 102–4, 125n.18;

possibilities for, 31–35, 47–48, 49–52, 99–100, 106–9
Dewey, John: compared to James, 16–19; and conceptual reconstruction, 52–55, 63–66, 83; on democracy, 56–58, 85–90; on faith and social reconstruction, 21, 93, 95–96, 102–9; general philosophical perspective of, 5–6, 116–17; general social philosophy of, 7–8, 18–19, 23, 38–58, 111
Dicker, Georges, 105

Edel, Abraham, 10
Ekirch, Arthur A., Jr., 91
Emerson, Ralph Waldo: individualism in, 14, 21–22; optimism in, 94–95, 102, 105; on social problems, 21–22, 25
Equality: and democracy, 8, 71–72, 85–90; importance of, 71
Ethics: of fulfillment, 10–12, 14–16, 21–22; of reform, 10–11, 13–19

Faith: importance to social reconstruction, 21, 30, 57–58, 102–9; justification of, 106–9
Fallibilism, 3, 11
Follett, Mary Parker, 87
Foster, William Zebulon, 24
Frankel, Charles, 39, 49
Freedom: as primary social value, 71–77; and democracy, 8, 71–72, 84–90; ever in process, 80–81, 82–83; overemphasis upon, 78–82
Frontier, 91–92

Garrison, George R., 14
God, 17, 68, 107–8

NOTE ON THE AUTHOR

JAMES CAMPBELL is Associate Professor of Philosophy at the University of Toledo. He received his Ph.D. in Philosophy from the State University of New York at Stony Brook. He is the author of a number of essays in American philosophy and intellectual history and the editor of the *Selected Writings of James Hayden Tufts.*